CW01184136

Plate I Excavations by the Kent Archaeological Rescue Unit in progress, 1988

FRONTISPIECE

THE ROMAN VILLA SITE AT ORPINGTON, KENT

The detailed report on the complete excavation of the Roman villa at Crofton, Orpington in 1988–9, its subsequent preservation and presentation to the public. It covers evidence of modest pre-Roman activity, five major periods of Roman construction and also of the lost late-Saxon settlement of Croctune.

by

BRIAN PHILP

With other main contributions by:

    John Willson   Peter Keller
    Joanna Bird   Kay Hartley
    Maurice Chenery

SEVENTH RESEARCH REPORT IN THE KENT MONOGRAPH SERIES
(ISSN 0141 22614)
(ISBN 0947831.13.4)

Published by: The Kent Archaeological Rescue Unit
Roman Painted House, New Street, Dover, Kent

All rights reserved. No part of this publication may be produced, stored in a retrieval system, or transmitted, in any form or by any means electronic, mechanical, photocopying, recording or otherwise, without the prior written consent of the Kent Archaeological Rescue Unit.

1996

Dedicated to the memory of

PETER (RICHARD) GRANT

for 25 years a dedicated amateur archaeologist working at Keston, Crofton and dozens of Bromley and Kent sites; an exemplary chairman of the Council for Kentish Archaeology (1986–1991) and a loyal and trusted friend.

Produced for the Unit by Alan Sutton Publishing Ltd., Stroud, Gloucestershire.

The Unit is greatly indebted to the **LONDON BOROUGH OF BROMLEY** for providing half of the printing costs of this Report and to the **KENT ARCHAEOLOGICAL TRUST and COUNCIL FOR KENTISH ARCHAEOLOGY** for their constant support.

CONTENTS

                                                                                     page

CHAPTER I   INTRODUCTION
- a) The Site   1
- b) Discovery   1
- c) The Complete Excavation in 1988–9   4
- d) Saving the Site from Destruction   5
- e) The Preservation Scheme   7
- f) Acknowledgements   8

CHAPTER II   THE EXCAVATED STRUCTURES AND FEATURES
- a) The pre-Villa Features   9
- b) The Roman Villa
    - Period I   :   A.D. 140–170   10
    - Period II   :   A.D. 170–200   15
    - Period III   :   A.D. 200–225   18
    - Period IV   :   A.D. 225–250   23
    - Period V   :   A.D. 270–300   25
    - Other Features and Deposits   36
- c) The Post-Roman Period   52

CHAPTER III   THE EXCAVATED OBJECTS
- a) The Coins   55
- b) The Small Finds   57
- c) The Samian Ware by Joanna Bird   62
- d) Potters' Stamps on Samian Ware by Brenda Dickinson   68
- e) The Mortaria by Kay Hartley   69
- f) The Coarse Pottery by Peter Keller   71
- g) The Painted Plaster   80
- h) The Other Objects   87
- i) Building Materials   88

CHAPTER IV   DISCUSSION   90

BIBLIOGRAPHICAL REFERENCES   96

INDEX   99

PLATES

LIST OF FIGURES

Fig.	1.	Map of south-east England, showing the Orpington area	2
Fig.	2.	Contour map of the Crofton area	3
Fig.	3.	Plan of the overall site showing limits of excavation	6
Fig.	4.	Site-plan showing Roman villa and related features	*facing* 28
Fig.	5.	Major sections across the Villa	*facing* 29
Fig.	6.	Sections across the Villa	*facing* 30
Fig.	7.	Sections across the Villa	*facing* 31
Fig.	8.	Sections across hypocaust channels, various rooms	31
Fig.	9.	Sections across shafts F51 and F58 (1/20)	35
Fig.	10.	Sections across Ditches and Gullies (1/20)	37
Fig.	11.	Sections across Pit-Line A (1/20)	39
Fig.	12.	Sections across Pit-Line B (1/20)	42
Fig.	13.	Sections across Pit-Line C (1/20)	44
Fig.	14.	Sections across Pit-Line D (1/20)	46
Fig.	15.	Sections across miscellaneous Pits and Post-holes (1/20)	47
Fig.	16.	Plans showing development of Villa, Periods I–V	54
Fig.	17.	Objects of bronze	56
Fig.	18.	Objects of bronze and bone	58
Fig.	19.	Objects of jet, shale, stone and glass	60
Fig.	20.	Objects of glass	61
Fig.	21.	Decorated samian ware and stamps	64
Fig.	22.	Mortaria	70
Fig.	23.	Coarse pottery	72
Fig.	24.	Coarse pottery	74
Fig.	25.	Coarse pottery	76
Fig.	26.	Coarse pottery	79
Fig.	27.	Painted wall plaster, designs on Fabric A	81
Fig.	28.	Painted wall plaster, designs on Fabric B	82
Fig.	29.	Painted wall plaster, designs on Fabric F	83
Fig.	30.	Painted wall plaster, designs on Fabric D	84
Fig.	31.	Area of fallen painted wall plaster, West Corridor	85
Fig.	32.	Reconstructed painted design, West Corridor	86

LIST OF PLATES

Plate I	Excavations by the Kent Archaeological Rescue Unit in progress, 1988 (frontispiece).
Plate II	Members of the public being given guided tours of the site, July, 1988.
Plate III	The rammed chalk foundations in Room 2 (Period I).
Plate IV	Section of collapsed wall of the West Corridor (by Room 7) sealing fallen roof tiles.
Plate V	Detail of splayed window-opening in collapsed West Corridor wall.
Plate VI	The north-west corner of Room 15, later cut by the Period V wall of Room 16 (at top).
Plate VII	Room 8, showing rammed chalk foundations (Period I), floor (Period II), side walls (Period III), fallen roof tiles and Shaft F 51 (bottom left).
Plate VIII	Room 9 from the north-east, showing west wall and floor (Period II), east wall (Period III) and south wall and stoke-hole (both Period V).
Plate IX	Detail showing rammed chalk foundations (Period I) under flint wall (Period III) on west side of Room 4.
Plate X	Detail of tiled base in stoke-hole Room 9.
Plate XI	Detail showing surviving area of tessellated floor in Room 11 (Period III).
Plate XII	South-west corner (with tiles) of Room 14C (Period IV) cutting through the south wall of Room 15 (Period II).
Plate XIII	General view from the north-east showing Rooms 11 (foreground), 13B (left), 14D (top), during Period V.
Plate XIV	General view from the east showing Rooms 5 (foreground), 6 (centre), 10 (top), 16 (top left) and 11 (left), during Period V.
Plate XV	Room 6B (Period V) from the north-east showing hypocaust channels.
Plate XVI	Room 10 (Period V) from the south-west showing pilae and main flue openings.
Plate XVII	Detail of north-west corner of Room 10 (Period V) showing pilae stacks, arched opening (right) and wall flues.
Plate XVIII	Detail showing tiled offset and box-flue tile in west wall of Room 10 (Period V).
Plate XIX	Room 16 (Period V) from the west showing dwarf walls and main flue (on left).
Plate XX	General view of surviving channelled hypocaust in Room 13B (Period V) from the north-west.
Plate XXI	Detail of hypocaust channels in Room 13B (Period V) showing chalk blocks and tiles.
Plate XXII	General view of Room 14D (Period V) from the north-west showing substantially complete hypocaust system.
Plate XXIII	Detail showing tiles covering the hypocaust channels at the centre of Room 14D (Period V).
Plate XXIV	Detail showing animal paw-prints on tiles built into the hypocaust in Room 14D (Period V).
Plate XXV	The West Ditch (fourth century) from the east, showing re-cut and earlier adjacent features (left).
Plate XXVI	Shaft F 51 (fourth century) fully excavated, cutting through the north wall of Room 8 (Period III).

Plate XXVII	Pit-Line B from the east, cutting through Gully F21, with Pit-Line C (left) and West Ditch (right).
Plate XXVIII	Detail showing area of fallen roof-tiles on west side of villa outside Room 9.
Plate XXIX	Detail showing section across 11–12th century hearth cut into hillwash layers sealing the Roman villa, with Post Hole F26 in foreground.

ABOUT THIS REPORT

This Report is the seventh in the Kent Monograph Series and it largely follows the pattern set by previous volumes. These were:-

Vol. I Excavations at Faversham 1965 (published by the C.K.A. in 1968).
Vol. II Excavations in West Kent 1960–70 (published by the Kent Unit in 1973).
Vol. III The excavation of the Roman Forts of the Classis Britannica at Dover 1970–77 (published by the Kent Unit in 1981).
Vol. IV Excavations in the Darent Valley, Kent (published by the Kent Unit in 1984).
Vol. V The Roman House with the Bacchic Murals at Dover (published by the Kent Unit in 1989).
Vol. VI The Roman Villa Site at Keston, Kent. First Report: Excavations 1968–78 (published by the Kent Unit in 1991).

As with all Reports in this series the entire proceeds from sales go towards covering the printing and publication costs, or into a reserve fund for subsequent volumes. No royalties are paid to any author. Further Reports are now in preparation.

The subject of this Report is the total excavation of the surviving section of the Roman villa site at Crofton, Orpington carried out jointly by the Kent Archaeological Rescue Unit and the Bromley and West Kent Archaeological Group. Short interim accounts have already appeared in the *Kent Archaeological Review* and other information is available on site during open-days (April – October each year).

The major features and structures are arranged here in chronological order by period, whilst the miscellaneous features are listed at the end of the main text. The key dating evidence is presented here and includes reports on all the coins and samian from the site, but only selective reports on the mortaria, small-finds, coarse pottery and painted plaster. Lack of resources has prevented a detailed study of the coarse pottery by fabric and the animal bones from the site were mostly unstratified. Over 100 soil-samples taken during the excavation are in store and have not been studied due to lack of funds.

As with previous Reports in this series, footnotes have been excluded and bibliographical references, numbered progressively throughout the text, are listed in that order at the back. These show as numbers placed in round-brackets and prefixed by the letters Ref. (e.g. (Ref. 47)). Similarly, the illustrated finds are also numbered progressively through the text, this time prefixed by the letters No. or Nos. so as to eliminate recurring finds-numbers and thus hopefully avoiding confusion. Coins (not illustrated) are noted in the text by a unique number (e.g. Coin No. 15) which refers to the number in the table of coins in the appropriate specialist section. References in the text to drawn sections and layers are shown in brackets, prefixed by the letters S. and L., respectively (e.g. S.4, L.3). A key covering all the published sections can be found on Fig. 5. The main text is set in 12 on 13 point Bembo typeface. The excavated features retain their original site feature number.

SUMMARY

Following its discovery in 1926 and limited excavation in 1955–61, the villa was fully excavated in 1988–9 by the Kent Archaeological Rescue Unit. A light scatter of struck flint, a gully and three minor features probably relate to an early prehistoric settlement. This stood in an elevated position on the west side of the Cray Valley.

About the middle of the 1st century A.D. a small farmstead, represented by an enclosure ditch, two small gullies, some pottery and a brooch, was established. About A.D. 140–170 (Period I) a sturdy rectangular villa, about 30 × 10.40 m. and covering about 310 sq. m., including four large rooms (Rooms 1–4), a smaller room (Room 5) and a flanking West Corridor, was constructed.

About A.D. 170–200 (Period II) the west wall of the villa had to be removed and its replacement made the corridor wider. The latter was then provided with both *opus signinum* and clay floors and its north end subdivided to create a small room (Room 7). Another room (Room 15), then added to the south-west corner, perhaps a kitchen, also had a thin *opus signinum* floor.

About A.D. 200–225 (Period IIIA) a major expansion changed the character of the building and increased its size to about 37.50 × 14.50 m. and its area to about 560 sq. m. A large south block was then added with three new rooms (Rooms 12, 13A and 14A), a passageway (Room 11) linking with the original building and a wide East Corridor down the length of the original house. Internally, Room 5 was subdivided (to form Room 6A) and the West Corridor blocked by two cross-walls, perhaps an entrance passage (Room 8). Plain tessellated floors were laid in Rooms 1, 2, 4, 5 and 11 and probably others. A small tank (Room 14B), or bath, was later (Period IIIB) inserted over Room 14A.

About A.D. 225–250 (Period IV) the old south-west extension (Room 15) was demolished and a new room (Room 14C) created to restore the original west alignment. About A.D. 270–300 (Period V) another major programme of building work drastically reduced the villa to about 20 × 14 m., about 280 sq. m. almost back to the size of the Period I house. The northern half of the building was abandoned and some of its materials used to construct a suite of five rooms (Rooms 6, 10, 16, 13B and 14D), all with deep hypocausts, at the south end. Room 9 was converted into a stoke-hole and part of its floor cut away. Domestic rubbish was dumped over the remains of the north rooms at this time and later in the 4th century a wide ditch and two abortive well-shafts were dug on the west side of the villa. The latest coins are of Arcadius and suggest that the villa was abandoned no later than the early-5th century.

During the villa's history many of its walls were decorated with painted designs, both geometric and three-dimensional, whilst some of the rooms were glazed. One room may have contained a small mosaic panel. The villa was clearly the main house of a major Roman estate and ancillary buildings, such as granary, bath-house and also at least one cemetery must have existed. The villa family probably farmed much of the Upper Cray valley and was one of the important land-owners in the Kent countryside.

Substantial wall-robbing took place before the abandoned villa was buried under deep layers of hillwash. The site was re-occupied about 11th–12th centuries and later, probably by the lost village of Croctune recorded in the Domesday Survey.

CHAPTER I

INTRODUCTION

A. THE SITE (FIGS. 1 AND 2)

The site (N.G.R. TQ 4542.6584) at Crofton lies within the parish of Orpington, about 1.5 km. south-west of the ancient parish church. Orpington, originally a Kent parish and later a substantial suburb, became part of Bromley a major S.E. London borough, in 1965. It occupies part of the Cray Valley close to a point where it leaves the North Downs. The River Cray flows north-east for about 13 km., in a steadily declining valley, where it joins the River Darent before flowing out into the River Thames.

The Roman villa at Crofton now lies protected within a substantial cover-building on the north side of Crofton Road, just above the terraced car park of Orpington B.R. Station. It occupied part of the steep upper slope of the hill forming the west side of the Cray valley at an elevation of about 88–90 m. O.D. The crest of the hill above is at about 106 m. and the adjacent valley bottom lies at about 58 m. This part of the valley is now dry, but it is highly likely that the River Cray flowed here in some quantity in Roman times.

The villa was built along the contours on an axis of about 030°, with the facade largely facing south-east towards the North Downs. Several minor Roman sites are known along the Lower Cray Valley and to the west in the old valley of the River Ravensbourne. Major Roman sites include the substantial villa complex at Warbank, Keston (Ref. 1), excavated by the writer in 1967–1992 and the Roman settlement at Fordcroft, Orpington/St. Mary Cray, excavated from 1965 onwards (Ref. 2). The Darent Valley lies only 8 km. to the east and this contains a series of substantial Roman villas, notably at Darenth (Ref. 3), Horton Kirby (Ref. 4), Farningham (Ref. 5) and Lullingstone (Ref. 6).

Roman *Londinium*, the provincial capital, lay only 19 km. to the north-west but there is no known road link with the site. The major Roman roads lay 7 km. to the west (London–Lewes) or 10 km. to the north (London–Dover, now the A2), whilst it is likely that the main local route was along the actual valley.

The area around the villa site was farmland for many centuries, but in about 1870 the South Eastern Railway was constructed, with a main station, only 80 m. east of the site. Later that century, a large cutting was made into the adjacent hill on the west side to form a related yard. It is now clear that this cutting removed the north end of the villa and also everything in front of it too. No records exist of what was then exposed and removed.

The whole area was heavily developed in about the 1930's when the villa site was largely enclosed by suburban housing. Crofton Road, called Pickingtons Lane on 19th century maps, is now much widened and a major traffic route (A 232).

B. DISCOVERY

The site was discovered accidentally late in November, 1926, when Council workmen were making two driveways leading to newly constructed Council Offices at Crofton Road, just above Orpington Railway Station. As they cut through a high bank on the north side of the road they smashed out several Roman walls and floors to achieve a convenient level. The site

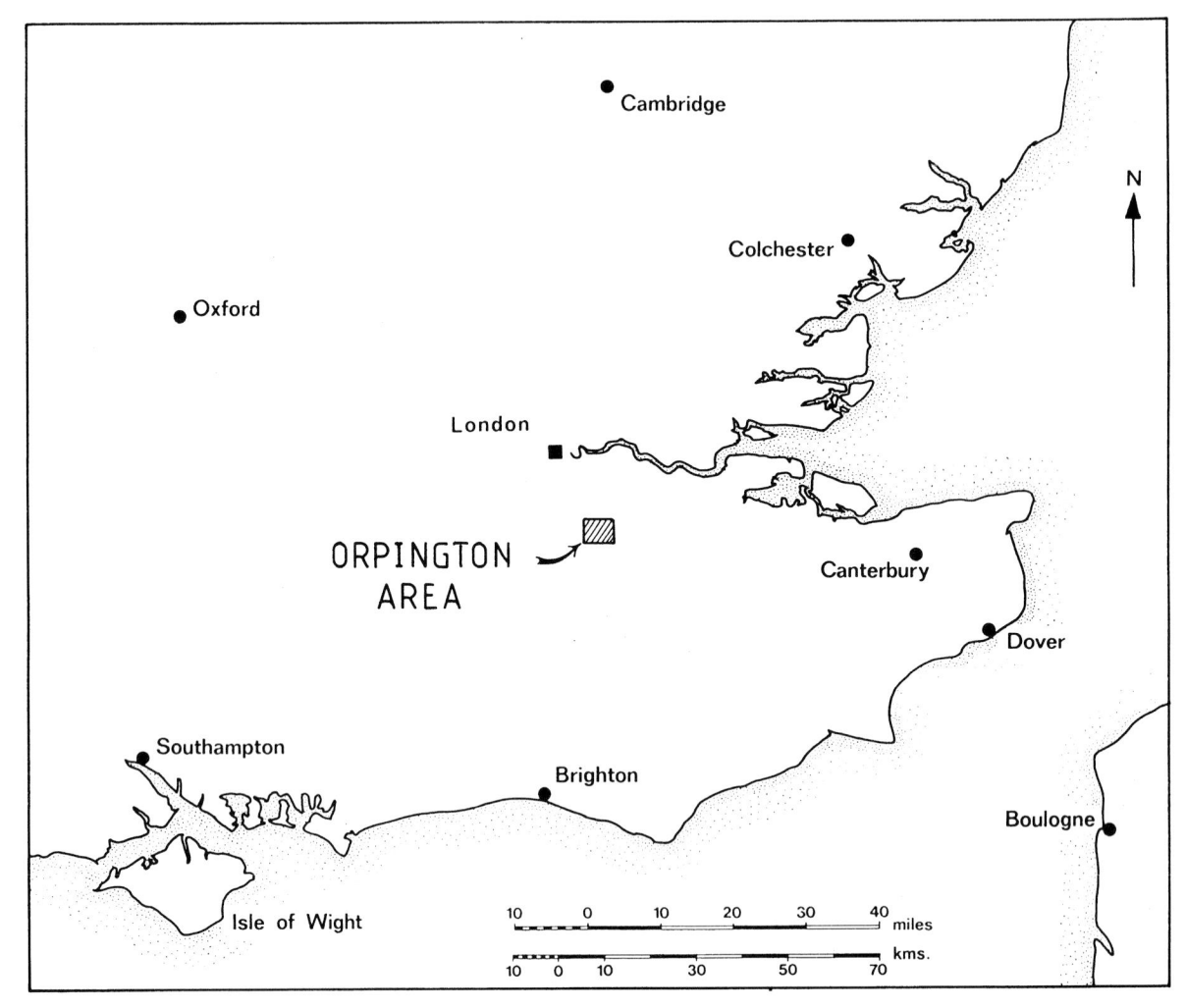

Fig. 1. Map of south-east England, showing the Orpington area

was first visited in January, 1927, (Ref. 7–9) by Mr. F. C. Elliston Erwood who had been carrying out excavations on sites in the Greenwich area for some years. He appealed for funds and on obtaining a small sum, he employed workmen on clearing parts of adjacent rooms. Some photographs survive showing walls, a substantially complete hypocaust arch, stacks of pilae tiles and large fragments of pottery. Undue publicity resulted in the site being badly damaged by treasure-hunters and the excavation was abandoned. The excavated areas were later backfilled and several wall-stubs left projecting from the banks on each side of the two driveways.

Thirty years later (1955–61) the site became the subject of a more careful excavation by members of the archaeological section of the Orpington Historical Records and Natural History Society, led by Mr. John Parsons. This work, largely carried out at weekends in 1955–57, had to be confined to narrow strips alongside the driveways. This work produced some important new information, but its publication was limited to brief annual notes (Ref. 10–12). It showed several structural changes, a certain hypocaust, two abandoned well-shafts and chalk foundations. The latest coin had been one of Arcadius (A.D. 383–408). Part of a glass cone-beaker and an iron knife were thought to be Anglo-Saxon. The work also suggested an Iron Age hut beneath the Roman floors and that the Villa was built about

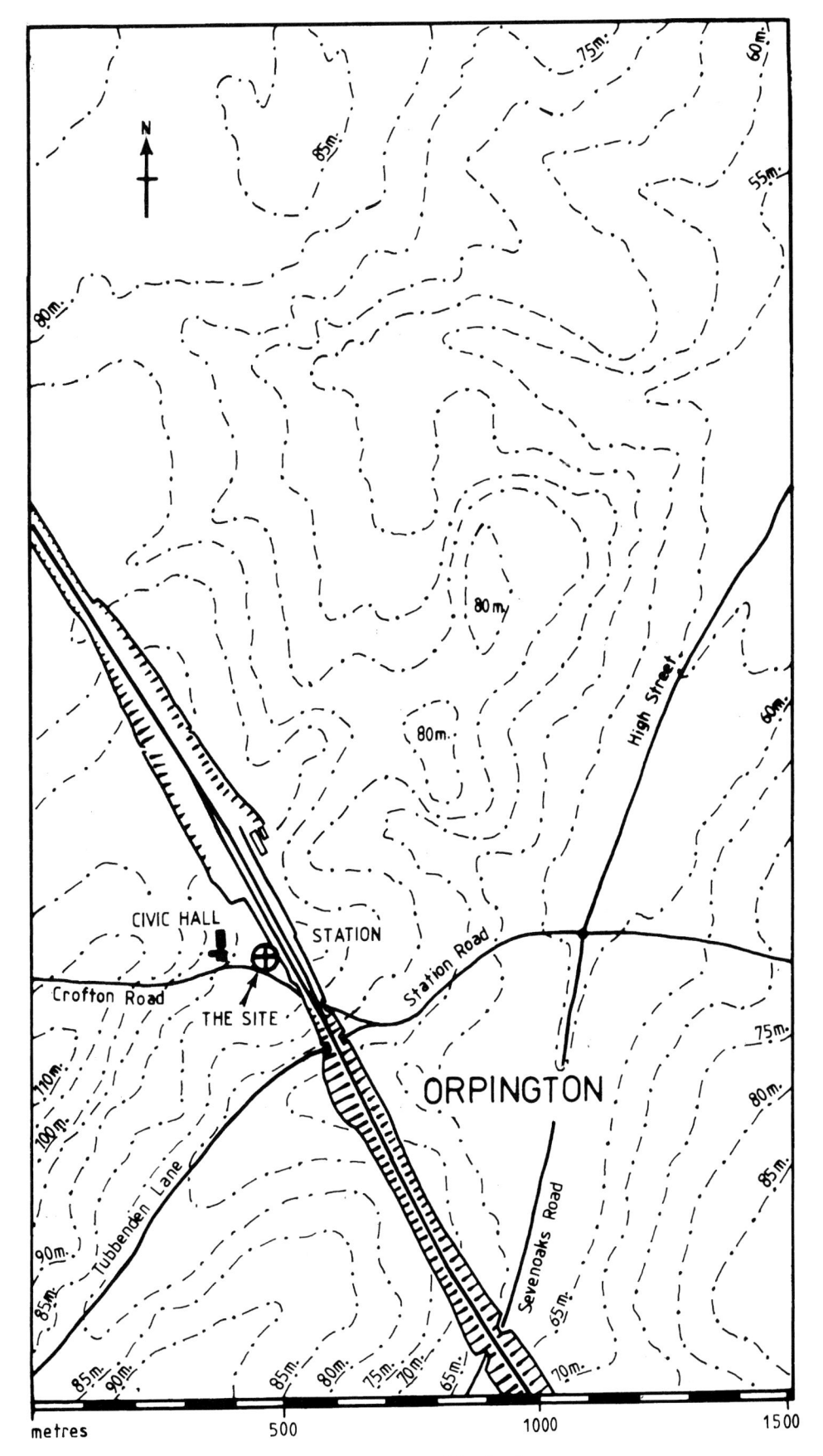

Fig. 2. Contour map of the Crofton area

A.D. 80, both matters disproved by the full excavation in 1988. Much later, a slightly expanded report and plan were published (Ref. 13) by Mr. Parsons. In 1984 (Ref. 14) the present writer published the original 1927 plan, given to him by Mr. Erwood before his death in 1968 and also summarised the information available at that time. The work in 1988 showed that both plans needed some correction.

The work initiated and directed by Mr. Parsons in the 1950's was well-organised and of a good general standard in its day. It also provided an important focus for archaeological activity in the Upper Cray Valley, much needed in the post-war years. It was one of Kent's pioneering projects, much like those at Lullingstone, Reculver and Springhead, all of which set the scene for later (and better funded) operations. Its common failing was that it was never taken through to full publication. These early projects, together with the interest which they generated, led to a rapid increase in archaeological knowledge and activity and which in 1964 led to the creation of the Council for Kentish Archaeology.

C. THE COMPLETE EXCAVATION IN 1988–9 (PLATE I)

The site of the villa remained buried and largely forgotten for many years, but gained total protection when it was scheduled as an Ancient Monument (London No. 115). In about 1983, however, the London Borough of Bromley which had inherited the site years before, sold off the old Council Offices and some adjacent land. This was bought by Baxter & Co. as their main office and the building named Lynwood House. The old Civic Halls remained behind the house and Bromley Council soon proposed a scheme to extend these and create large adjacent car parks. This included the whole area occupied by the villa and an application was soon made to English Heritage for the removal of the villa. Consent was granted (on 25th August, 1987) for this destruction on the grounds that the villa had already been substantially destroyed. A condition, however, required that the K.A.R.U. should be allowed to excavate the site ahead of the building programme.

As a result the Unit began work in May, 1988, when a maximum of 12 weeks was allowed, with funding provided by the London Borough of Bromley. Some 300 tons of topsoil, tree roots, rubbish and sterile hillwash was removed by machine and taken away by lorry. Hand-excavation by a large team soon revealed many features outside and north of the Roman house, besides clear evidence of extensive surviving masonry. In early July it was possible to give guided tours to 800 local school children and by mid-July it was clear that what survived was substantial. As a result (see below) the programme was changed and work continued until about mid-November, when the work had been in progress non-stop for 130 days. A large team from the Bromley and West Kent Archaeological Group joined in throughout the six months and another group from Orpington and District Archaeological Society was able to work in May and June.

The work in 1988 excavated most of the Roman building, compiled a detailed written and photographic record and recovered a substantial number of objects (Ref. 15). A small team had to return in September and October, 1989 to complete the excavation of the south-west corner of the villa on private land which had previously been unavailable. The limits of the areas excavated are shown on the overall site-plan (Fig. 3).

The total archive for the site includes about 50 boxes of objects recovered from the excavations and these are now deposited with Bromley Museum at Orpington. The written archive includes 14 plans, over 130 sections, 10 folders and over 500 photographs and slides. In all some 453 individual deposits were recorded and this number would have been much greater, but for the several earlier disturbances.

The cost of the excavation was about £12,000 and the post-excavation work about £8,000. This was provided by the London Borough of Bromley under the Consent given by English Heritage. The report-writing and preparation cost about £8,000 and this had to be provided by the Kent Unit. The publication and editing costs totalled more than £10,000 and this was shared jointly by the London Borough of Bromley and the Kent Unit.

The finds from the 1955–61 excavation were kindly made available by Mr. Parsons in 1990, after years of storage in at least two places. Most of this was in a wide range of small boxes, cartons and paper bags. Some had been marked and some had not. The Unit placed the whole collection into clean plastic bags, where possible keeping related groups together. In all some 65 bags were used and these placed in four long-bone boxes marked "J. Parsons Collection", Boxes 1–4.

A preliminary examination showed that a large amount of work would have been involved in trying to match-up soil deposits across a span of over 30 years. Some of the material would have to be treated as unstratified and in general it largely matched the much greater collection from the large-scale 1988–89 excavation. It mostly included coarse pottery and bone, but several pieces of samian, glass and about 20 struck flint flakes were also included. Significantly, it also included two small white tesserae and one large buff-coloured tessera. These special finds were rebagged and placed in a box marked No. 5.

D. SAVING THE SITE FROM DESTRUCTION

By mid-July it was becoming clear that the villa-house was not only more extensive than previously supposed, but that what survived was also substantially more complete. As a result the Kent Unit explained the matter to Council officers and to the site architects, all of whom readily responded and began to look at alternative arrangements. The Unit also sought the support of Bromley councillors in the hope that any suggested modifications to the car park might be approved. These moves were keenly supported by the Council for Kentish Archaeology, whose chairman Mr. Peter Grant, wrote to the chairman of the appropriate Bromley committee. In addition, Viscount Monckton of Brenchley, a Kent archaeologist in his own right, kindly visited the site and added his support. So, too, did Ivor Stanbrook, M.P. for Orpington, who visited the site early one Saturday morning and agreed that the villa was important to the constituency.

On the very last day of July it was possible, again with the agreement of Bromley Council, to open the site for a grand open-day for the public (Plate II). This was advertised locally and thanks to good weather more than 2,000 people poured onto the site in about six hours. This meant there were never less than 300 people on the site at any one time and it took six guides all their time to take large parties round. Another ten diggers had to act as marshalls and another 15 carried on with the actual digging under the close gaze of hundreds. Everyone visiting showed a great interest in the work and discoveries and subsequently many wrote helpful letters to Bromley Council to encourage the preservation of the site. In addition, two large groups of the Friends of C.K.A. were given special guided tours on other days.

All this helpful official and private interest resulted in the Recreation Committee of Bromley Council readily agreeing, at its meeting on 18th August, 1988 that the car park could be changed and the main part of the villa saved from destruction! This news was welcomed all round. The architects had come up with acceptable modifications and all interests were met. A victory for Bromley and the environment and an example for other local authorities to follow. Indeed, such was the interest of Bromley Council and its officers, that at a meeting of its Policy and Resources Committee held on 24th August, it was agreed in principle that a protective

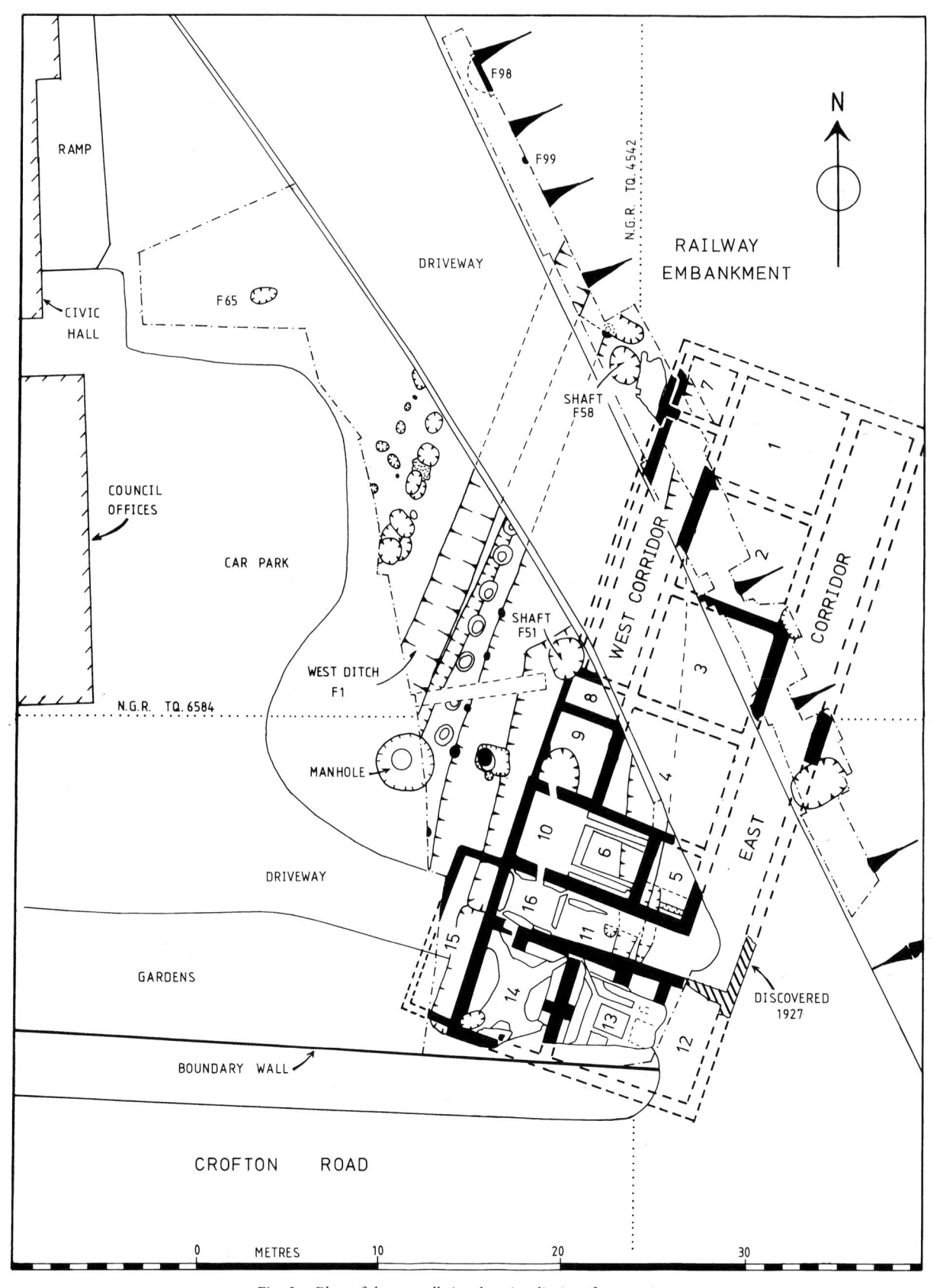

Fig. 3. Plan of the overall site showing limits of excavation

cover-building could be placed over the masonry to make it permanently available to the public. This, of course, subject to various local agreements and conditions.

On completion of the excavation the walls were sheeted over with plastic and some 300 tons of sand poured into the site to restore the area to its original level. This protected the walls from the weather, possible vandalism and vegetation for the next three years, including during the whole of the building programme.

E. THE PRESERVATION SCHEME

Once the decision to save the villa and open it for permanent public inspection had been made, the whole matter lost its on-site impetus. Detailed discussions and meetings followed throughout 1989 and by the end of April, 1990, the project was finally agreed. This followed a design, layout and programme, produced by the Kent Unit and work started on 8th May, 1990 (Ref. 17). The whole project was then undertaken by the Kent Unit which did the bulk of the work ably assisted by the Bromley and West Kent Archaeological Group, only using sub-contractors where this was essential. The total cost was estimated at £83,000.

The initial tasks were to clear the site, mark out the building, cut deep foundation-trenches and pour in some 80 tons of concrete. Sub-contracting bricklayers constructed the footings and Unit staff then set all the steel and cast the final concrete ring-beam. The next major task was the construction of a large steel, portal-frame building, about 50 × 15 m. in size, fabricated in the Midlands and constructed by the suppliers. This was clad with carefully selected pebble-dash wall panels on two sides and profiled sheeting on the low-pitched roof. The Unit then supervised the cavity-wall brick infilling of two more sides and the insertion of three double doors and 22 windows. It then provided all the underground services, window glazing, internal lighting, extractor fan and welding of steel roof-brackets. By the end of October the building was weatherproof and watertight so that the next, indoor phase could begin. All this was completed in 170 days of non-stop work (Ref. 18).

The next phase was the re-excavation of 300 tons of soil placed over the villa to protect it from weather and the building works. This long task was followed by consolidation work on the Roman building, laying of internal floors, the wall-lining, barriers, displays, graphics, notices and external paving. These tasks were undertaken at intervals in 1991, following bureaucratic delays and some dragged on until 1992. Finally, the whole scheme was completed by June, 1992 and arrangements then agreed for the provisional opening to the public in September and October 1992 (Ref. 19). This proved highly successful and the villa was opened for a full season (April to October) in both 1993 and 1994. This was done under an agreement, whereby the Unit carried out the total management of the scheme on behalf of the London Borough of Bromley. The formal opening ceremony took place on 7th April, 1993. The final cost, external delays considered, was about £85,000.

Whilst the eventual outcome proved highly beneficial to the citizens of Bromley, the whole process from start to finish actually took four years of very hard work. Even though the outcome had provided satisfaction in itself it was additionally helpful that the scheme won high awards. Initially, in 1989 the Kent Archaeological Trust gave the London Borough of Bromley an award for preservation following its agreement to reduce the car park and thus save the villa from destruction (Ref. 16). In 1994 the scheme was entered for the British Archaeological Awards, held at York in November that year. The scheme won (jointly with another) the first prize for the Best Presentation of an Archaeological Project to the Public, securing a fine plaque, a cheque for £500 and a certificate, all presented and sponsored by The Virgin Group. It won an highly commended certificate, effectively the second prize, for

Best Project Securing the Long-term Preservation of a site, this time sponsored by English Heritage (Ref. 20).

F. ACKNOWLEDGEMENTS

Whilst the Unit Director led the project from start to finish he wishes to acknowledge, first and foremost, the hard work of many people with the various aspects of the project. Firstly, for those taking an important part in the excavations in 1988 and 1989. Here thanks are due to the supervisors Derek Garrod, Maurice Chenery and Barry Corke who were largely responsible for the detailed site-recording and planning. Next to some 30 members of the Kent Unit, some 20 members of the Bromley and West Kent Group and another six members of the Orpington and District Archaeological Society. Of all these Messrs. Tom Tasker, Maurice Godfrey, Peter Grant, Len Johnson, Alan Morley, Gerry Geradine, Michael Meekums, Will Foot, Jan Mondrejewski, Keith Parfitt, Julian Bird, Phil Winter, Mike Bennett and also Audrey Button, Pat Crozier, Sue Macpherson and Valerie Satterthwaite must be thanked for work over extended periods.

Secondly, thanks are also due to those helping with the building programme and presentation scheme. In addition to Maurice Chenery and Barry Corke, Maurice Godfrey played an important role here, supported at different times by Peter Grant, Audrey Button, Mike Bennett, Christine Pegram, Alan Morley, Len Johnson, Will Foot and Gerry Geradine, all of whom made substantial contributions to the project.

Thirdly, the financial support and goodwill of the Council of the London Borough of Bromley, notably from Councillor Mr. R. Foister and its Leisure Services Committee; later Barry Walkinshaw and Alan Tyler, of the Leisure Services Dept., gave their helpful support.

Fourthly, the preparation of this Report has required further substantial input by many more people. Dr. R. Reece has kindly dated the coins; Joanna Bird has kindly examined and dated the samian ware; Kay Hartley has kindly dated the mortaria; Keith Parfitt has described the small-finds and Peter Keller has written the coarse pottery catalogue. John Willson has kindly drawn all the illustrated pottery; Wendy Williams kindly drew the small-finds; John Willson and Maurice Chenery drew all the plans and sections, whilst the latter and Mrs. Pam Barrett greatly assisted with the classification and typing, respectively. Miss Audrey Button has also very kindly read the text and suggested various improvements.

CHAPTER II

THE EXCAVATED STRUCTURES AND FEATURES

A. PRE-VILLA FEATURES (FIG. 4)

Several features were found on the site that clearly pre-dated the Roman walls and floors. These are described below.

GULLY F102

This small gully was found under Room 5 on an east–west axis. It was traced for a distance of only about 1.50 m., with both ends cut away, its west end by a small ditch (F104). It was about 30 cm. wide, about 15 cm. deep and V-shaped in profile. Its filling consisted of a light brown sandy loam. This produced a single sherd of a large storage jar, with chevron decoration, found in late-1st century contexts on some West Kent sites.

SMALL DITCH F104 (FIG. 7, S.15).

This was traced under Rooms 5 and 11 running on a north–south axis. Neither end was found and its minimum length was 7.65 m.; its width varied from 25–65 cm. Its depth varied from 25–34 cm. and it was U-shaped in profile. It cut Gully F102, but was in turn cut by the Early Ditch F101. Its filling consisted of sandy loams with occasional pebbles and the only finds were two waste flint flakes and four heat-cracked stones.

THE EARLY DITCH F59 AND F101 (FIG. 7, S.15).

This was found beneath Rooms 4, 5, 6, 7, 11 and the West Corridor for a minimum of 30.50 m., on a roughly north–south axis. Its north end had been removed by the railway cutting and its southern end was probably removed when the south wall of Room 11 was constructed. No traces of this ditch were found in the 5 m. to the south and it seems likely that it actually terminated before it reached Room 13. It varied in width from 1.05–2.00 m. and in depth from 40–76 cm. It had a broad upper profile, but had a narrow U-shaped base. The filling consisted of sandy loams and clays. It cut a smaller ditch, F104. This linear ditch was originally located in 1926 and again in 1956 when it was seen obliquely alongside the drive and then thought to be a section across a prehistoric hut. With the complete excavation in 1988 it is now certain that this was not a hut, but a linear ditch.

Its filling produced 12 potsherds, four struck waste flint flakes and 21 fire-cracked flints. The pottery includes the base of a thick grog-tempered storage jar, sherds of two comb-decorated cooking-pots and a fine vessel with corrugations on the shoulder, all four of mid-1st century date. A small sherd of a coarse flint-tempered vessel and part of a fine ware bowl, could both be pre-Conquest. The latest two vessels are the rim (No. 72) of a small cooking pot and a sherd of a burnished cooking pot. These seem to date from about A.D. 80–130, which taken with the lack of Antonine pottery so abundant elsewhere on the site, suggests it was filled no later than about A.D. 130.

GULLY F21

A straight, shallow gully was located over a distance of 12.80 m. at a point about 6 m. west of the Roman house. Neither end was found, but it had sloping sides and a rounded base. It was generally 0.75 m. wide, 30 cm. deep and was filled with a sandy grey-brown loam. No pottery, tile or any object of Roman date was found in it and the only finds were eight struck flints and three fire-cracked stones. It was cut by several of the pits in Pit-Line B and it is likely that this was a feature of prehistoric date. It is possible that it related to the area of fire-cracked stones (F13) and its three adjacent pits (see below).

PRE-VILLA SOILS (FIGS. 5 AND 7)

It is clear that the underlying natural Thanet Beds, here yellow-brown sand and clays, was capped by a substantial deposit of fine light brown sandy loam. This seems to represent the pre-Roman soils and it was into this deposit that the pre-villa features (see above) and the Period I rammed chalk foundations (see below) had been dug.

This primary deposit had been substantially removed in many places by the construction of hypocausts (in Rooms 6, 10, 16, 13C and 14D) or by terraces on the west side, including that for Room 15. Small isolated sections were examined in some places under the main Roman building, but on the east side this layer was substantially intact (S.2. L.5 and S4. L5) where there was less need to reduce it owing to the downward slope of the hill. Other areas within the building remain sealed by later floors (notably in Rooms 8, 9, 4 and 5), which were not removed during the excavation. In some places the primary soil was sealed by a second, distinctive layer of brown loam (S.14. L.8–9 and S.16. L5) which may represent soil upcast spread around when the Period I foundation-trenches were dug.

In these pre-villa soils were some 37 potsherds, 59 struck flints and 43 fire-cracked flints. The sherds are mostly native wares, including shell and grog-tempered fabrics, perhaps cooking pots of 1st century A.D. date. About 15 are hard, sandy fabrics which include sherds of a lid, a poppy-head beaker, cooking pots, a beaker and two flagons. Whilst some of these may be dated to the second half of the 1st century A.D., several others are likely to be of 2nd century date. Nothing need be any later than A.D. 130, as Antonine pottery so abundant on the site, is absent!

The same primary and upcast soils were found beyond the villa-house on the north and west sides, but these were not sealed by floors. They must have remained open during the early years of the villa itself. Here one brooch (No. 4), some 95 sherds, six flint flakes and two fire-cracked flints were found, of which four vessels (Nos. 55, 73–75) are illustrated.

The majority of the pottery is grog-tempered or sandy wares, the former including some Patch Grove pottery and there is also a little shell-loaded ware. The majority seems to be of 2nd century date, but earlier bead rim jars and cooking pots are again present. The later-2nd century pottery includes two bead rim dishes and two sharply everted rim jars.

Seven samian ware sherds represent five vessels, including a Form 30, or 37 and three of Form 31. All these are of Antonine date and it is clear from the pottery evidence that these soil deposits were still unsealed as late as about A.D. 200, but probably not later.

B. THE ROMAN VILLA

PERIOD I

It is clear that the early features on the site were eventually superseded by a substantial masonry building, expanded and developed over a period of at least two hundred years. It is also clear that the primary structure on this site was a basic rectangular building consisting of at least five large rooms and a West Corridor (Period I). This was characterised, uniquely on this site, by substantial rammed chalk foundations.

Although cut through by the 1926 driveway diagonally across its centre, sufficient survived on both sides to produce an acceptable plan. Whilst the south end seems to be clear, the north end extends beyond the edge of the railway cutting for an unknown distance. From what survives, the length is likely to have been about 30 m. and the width about 10.40 m. and the total area about 310 sq. m. (Fig. 16).

It is clear from what survives that Room 5 measured about 5.80 × 3.75 m. and Room 2 about 5.80 × 5.44 m. The West Corridor had an internal length of about 28.00 m. and an internal width of about 2.40 m. It is also clear that Room 4 was at least 4.50 m. wide. If it and Room 3 had been the same width (also about 5.50 m.), then the available space between Rooms 2 and 5 would have been equally divided. This would have created two more rooms (Rooms 3 and 4) and also allowed for an intermediate wall between them, as shown on the plan. By the same token, Room 1 must have extended at least 4.50 m. northwards, to match the minimum length of the corridor wall and quite likely it also had a similar width of 5.50 m., as suggested for the other rooms. This produces a sensible plan comprising four large rooms of equal size, with a smaller room at the south end and a West Corridor flanking all five rooms. Whilst doorways may have existed between each pair of rooms, it is equally likely that doorways led from each room into the wide corridor.

The rammed chalk foundations had been laid in vertically-sided trenches mostly 30–40 cm. deep. Those for the external West Corridor wall were mostly 55 cm. wide, those for the main structure were mostly 58–60 cm. wide, whilst the internal foundations for the rooms had been reduced to about 50 cm. These foundations only survived in disconnected lengths, due to the construction of the drives in 1926, mostly beneath later walls and for a total length of about 50 m. In several places these foundations supported mortared flint walls about 50–60 cm. wide. No details of the rest of the Period I structure are known for these were mainly superseded by later rebuilding (Periods II-V).

As regards dating evidence there was little associated with the construction of the Period I walls and foundations. Clearly, however, these were built prior to Periods II-V and later than the soil and features through which they had been built. These contained a small amount of pottery dating up to about A.D. 130 and Period I cannot be earlier than this. Of considerable importance, however, is the very large amount of samian ware and coarse pottery dating from the Antonine period (A.D. 140–180) which had been discarded as rubbish on the site. The greater part of this was recovered from the wide Early Terrace immediately behind the villa which had been cut to provide access at the rear of the building. There can be little reasonable doubt that this sudden influx of quantities of Antonine pottery onto the site relates to the Period I structure. On the total evidence this may be dated to about A.D. 140–170. As such, it can be regarded as a major rural development of the Antonine period.

Room 1
This room was almost totally destroyed by the railway cutting. Only short stubs of the foundations of its west and south walls were found, both badly damaged by the railway works. The presence of a substantial room here is anyway implied by the adjacent West Corridor, which clearly extends northwards for at least another 4 m. This corridor flanked the other rooms in the central block of the house and it clearly flanked Room 1 as well. On the assumption that the rooms with chalk foundations in the central block (all Period I) were of equal size, as the evidence suggests, then Room 1 was probably about 5.80 × 5.40 m. in extent. More than this cannot be said.

Room 2 (Plate III and Fig. 5. S.2)

Substantial parts of both the north-west and south-east corners of this room survived and these are sufficient to show that the room was originally 5.80 × 5.44 m., within the foundations. The foundations were of rammed chalk, clearly Period I, 50 cm. wide on the internal wall and up to 60 cm. wide on the main west wall. Although 5 m. of the south foundation and 4.50 m. of the west foundation were found, traces of the actual masonry only survived for about half this distance. The rest seems to have been removed following earlier archaeological work on the site. The wall generally survived only one or two courses high and this was built of flints set in a grey-white mortar, mostly 54 cm. wide.

Of the interior of this room only a strip barely 1.50 m. wide survived intact. This showed the pre-villa soils which must have formed the Period I floor, overlaid by a massive floor, probably laid in Period III. The latter was based on a foundation of large flints, with chalk, mortar and tile lumps, mostly 13 cm. thick. A thick layer of light concrete, 10 cm. thick and composed of cream-white mortar containing many small pebbles was then laid on the foundation. On this was laid a layer of *opus signinum*, up to 4 cm. thick, into which coarse plain red tesserae had been set to form a finished floor. Only a small patch of about 40 tesserae survived and this shows that the floor of Room 2 had been about 10 cm. higher than the clay floor in the adjacent West Corridor.

The floor was in a poor state and cut away in several places. The only significant feature was a small pit (F90), cut through the floor in late-Roman times which was found to contain a complete, coarse pottery vessel (No. 159). This was in an upright position and clearly quite deliberately placed, but nothing was found in or associated with it to suggest a function. On its merits it resembles a cremation-burial, or votive-deposit, but neither is proven and the pot was almost certainly buried in the 4th century when the northern end of the building had been abandoned and had, at least, partially collapsed.

Room 3

Only substantial lengths of the north and east foundation of this room survived, at the north-east corner. The north wall was shared with Room 2 (see above) and some 4.60 m. survived of the east wall. Most of this was rammed chalk foundation, mostly 50 cm. wide, but 1.40 m. of the actual wall survived. This was 58 cm. in width and built of flints, with occasional chalk blocks set in a grey-white mortar. It survived only two courses high.

No floor survived in this room and only a small 2 m. section of soil was left. This showed the primary pre-villa soils capped by a 25 cm. layer of flint, chalk lumps and tile fragments. This seems to represent a badly damaged floor sequence as found in Room 2. This is to some extent confirmed by the presence here of 69 (loose) plain red tesserae, similar to those from Rooms 2 and 4. Little else can be said.

Room 4 (Fig. 5, S.3)

Only small sections of the south and west walls of this room survived, the bulk having been removed by the construction of the driveway in 1926. The rammed chalk foundations, in one place 58 cm. wide and 38 cm. deep, were again present and of integral build at the south-west corner. These were typical of the Period I arrangements, but little trace of the Period I walls remained. In spite of damage, Room 4 must have occupied the whole width of the block, here clearly about 5.80 m. At least 4.50 m. of its width survived and if it largely matched Rooms 1, 2 and 3 (as seems likely), then its original width must have been about 5.50 m.

The walls over the chalk foundations are mostly those of Period III, a major rebuilding programme. These survived five courses high in places and consist of neatly coursed flints set in a buff mortar and pebbles and some 60 cm. in width. Of special interest is the fact that the

Period III west wall had been moved some 12 cm. eastwards of the chalk foundations, probably an error in marking out.

The primary pre-villa soils (L.15) and early ditch (F101) were found under this room and it is again likely that the Period I floor was of trodden soil. What is certain is that the solid floor in this room butted against the Period III wall and therefore cannot relate to Periods I or II. The floor had a base (L.10) of chalk and flint rubble, mostly 3–8 cm. thick and consisted of a weak concrete (L.9) of white mortar and pebbles 7–10 cm. thick. This was capped by a thin layer of *opus signinum* on which plain red floor tesserae had been bedded. About 10 tesserae survived *in situ*, though the 1927 plan shows many more. All the deposits above the finished floor had been removed by the earlier excavations.

Room 5 (Fig. 7, S.16)
Only sections of the four walls of this room had survived to varying degrees. The rammed chalk foundations of Period I were seen on the north, south and east sides, but they were absent under the west wall which was clearly inserted during the Period III rebuilding. It seems clear from this that originally Room 5 occupied the whole width of the main block, at about 5.80 m., but that it was only 3.75 m. across and was thus much smaller than the other Period I rooms (Rooms 1–4).

The only certain trace of the actual Period I wall was found on the east side where it was constructed of flint set in buff mortar and was 60 cm. in width. The Period III wall sat directly on this. The latter period also saw the insertion of a cross-wall dividing Room 5 into two unequal parts (hence Room 6). The foundations of the new wall cut deeply into the fill of the Early Ditch (F101), but the wall proper was 52 cm. wide and built of flints set in a pale buff mortar and pebbles. The room so created was 3.75 × 2.45 m. wide and composed of flints in buff mortar, surviving three courses high. This sat on a flint and loam foundation 40 cm. high, resting on the Period I chalk foundations. The south wall was the most complete and here the new wall was again 60 cm wide.

The primary soils (L.7) and Early Ditch (F101) had been cut through here by the chalk foundations and again the Period I floor must have been of trodden soil. The extant floor again relates to the Period III walls to which it butts and consists of a base (L.3) of flints, chalk lumps, pebbles, loam and mortar, generally 16 cm. thick. On this was laid a 2–4 cm. layer of pink *opus signinum* into which were set plain red tesserae. About 15 still survived, but many more remained *in situ* in 1927.

West Corridor (Fig. 5. S.1).
The overall excavation in 1988 revealed that most of the original West Corridor had been badly damaged by a variety of processes and that only a small section at the edge of the railway cutting had survived together with its related stratigraphy. The southern section of the corridor had been removed during the Period V rebuilding programme (Rooms 10 and 16) and the adjacent section deleted during the Period II alterations (Rooms 8 and 9). The driveway had removed another section some 8 m. in length in 1926.

The surviving section clearly revealed (Fig. 5) that the Period I chalk foundations, here containing some flint, had survived on both the west and east sides. They were 56 cm. and 60 cm. wide, respectively and the width of the corridor between them was 2.40 m. No trace of a corresponding constructed floor was found and it seems clear that the natural soils (L.29) here formed the actual surface. The internal Period I west wall was built of flints set in a hard grey-white mortar with fine flint grits. It was 52 cm. in width, had a narrow mortar spread along its north side and survived two courses high.

The excavation also revealed clear evidence of the Period II alterations. The narrower external west wall had been removed completely and replaced by a poor quality external wall built of chalk blocks, flints and large tile fragments set in buff mortar. This new wall was only 45 cm. in width and had been positioned some 40–50 cm. to the west, thus increasing the width of the corridor to about 3 m. It overlapped the abandoned Period I chalk foundations by only about 10–12 cm.

The new arrangements included a floor of brown clay at the north end, mostly 2–3 cm. in thickness, traced for a maximum of 4 m. and which very clearly sealed the abandoned Period I foundation and butted to the new Period II wall. Of special interest were the two linear slots associated with the floor that seem to have contained rectangular, horizontal beams. These cut across the corridor but were not quite parallel, being 1.10–1.25 m. apart. The beams may have been about 30 cm. wide and perhaps 25 cm. deep. The function of beams in this position is difficult to gauge, but they could have supported vertical partitions or could have formed floor-joists to take planks. Either way, they seem to have rotted and the soils above slumped into the cavities.

The corridor was also interrupted by the insertion of a cross-wall containing a doorway which seems to have created a small end room (Room 7). The new cross-wall (also Period II) was 84 cm. in length, 40 cm. wide and survived to a height of about 34 cm. (four courses). It was also built of mortared tile and flint. The end of the wall was finished with a narrow *opus signinum* moulding at floor-level, about 5 cm. high, 8 cm. wide and 34 cm. in length. This marked the door opening of which only 1.15 m. survived in the excavation. Significantly, the clay floor also covered the door opening which shows it also related to Period II. One beam-slot flanked the cross-wall on its southern side.

Close examination of the cross-wall showed that its south face at floor-level was plastered and painted with vertical red bands on a white background. A large section of similar plaster had fallen from the adjacent wall onto the clay floor with its painted surface downwards. This showed a rectilinear pattern of red panels, lined in green on a white ground (see Figs. 31–2). This collapse must mark the initial decay of the West Corridor at this point for it lay directly on the clay floor and no attempt had been made to clear it away. Some of the plaster had slumped into the void of the beam-slot, perhaps following the decay of the beam.

What is clear is that the northern end of the West Corridor was certainly abandoned, in common with the northern half of the building. The main evidence for this was the discovery of a long 4.00 m. section of the outer corridor wall, some 11 courses and 1.60 m. in extent, collapsed horizontally to the west (Plate IV). This sealed a substantial layer of roof tiles which had slid off prior to the collapse of the wall. The wall contained part of a splayed window (see below). The secondary evidence here took the form of deep layers of dumped soil, mostly 15–20 cm. deep containing domestic rubbish, fragments of wall plaster and some light building debris. It also included glass (No. 33) and a jet object (No. 26). This sealed the Period II clay floor and also the articulated layer of fallen plaster. The pottery from these dumps consists of about 250 potsherds representing at least 35 vessels (Nos. 76–82). These include four samian vessels dated Antonine-mid 3rd century and a mortarium (No. 65) dated A.D. 240–300. The coarse pottery includes four straight-sided dishes (A.D. 200–250), three flanged bowls (A.D. 250–300), three colour-coated beakers (A.D. 260–300) and one Farnham ware vessel (probably 4th century). From this it seems clear that this section of the West Corridor was being buried by dumps of domestic rubbish in the late-3rd and 4th centuries. Significantly, these dumps also sealed part of the collapsed Period II wall. The abandonment of the northern half of the building certainly relates to the major building works at the southern end of the building (Period V). The large amount of domestic rubbish dumped over the northern end of the building must, therefore, relate to Period V and strongly suggests that it dated to about A.D. 250–280 onwards.

The fallen walls and dumped soils containing the pottery were eventually sealed by a layer of soil up to 25 cm. deep containing large pieces of flint, chalk, mortar, *opus signinum* and tile. This seems to represent the final demolition of the Roman house perhaps taking place after the end of the 4th century.

The Early Terrace (Fig. 5, S.1)
This major feature, forming a marked terrace cut on the west side of the Roman house, had a minimum length of 30 m. Neither end was found. It had been cut into the hillside, some 40–50 cm. in depth and had a width of 3.70–4.50 m. Its cut face sloped gently uphill and its base was largely flat. It seems highly likely that this terrace was cut to provide a level access at the back of the Period I and Period II building.

The base of the terrace contained yellow-brown sandy loams (L.17–27), mostly without building debris. The deposits above this were grey-brown loams, with some flint, tile and mortar debris and domestic rubbish. These soils suggest progressive dumping which ultimately filled the terrace. These were substantially truncated when the Late Terrace was cut for the Period V building programme. These terraces seem to have provided a narrow-rear zone behind the house, which prevented storm-water reaching the building and allowed access. Pit-line B, about one metre beyond the lip of the terrace, may represent a substantial fence protecting both the terrace and the back of the building. The smaller, flint-packed post-holes (Pit-line C) seem to run along the lip of the terrace and may have formed a smaller fence retaining the bank and preventing access from outside.

As regards dating, a very large collection of pottery was recovered from some 27 deposits within the terrace. Some fragments from the same vessel occur in different deposits. In all about 3700 sherds (Nos. 83–94) were recovered including over 100 sherds of samian ware (Nos. 39 and 42) and mortaria (No. 64). Small-finds include bronze items (Nos. 7, 13 and 14), bone objects (Nos. 21–24), a stone tool (No. 29) and the base of a glass bottle (No. 32).

The coarse pottery is very largely 2nd century and mostly Antonine in date. 1st century pottery is largely absent, though some bead rim cooking-pots could be late-1st or early-2nd century. Patch Grove ware is present, mostly bowls or storage jars, whilst a range of other bowls, beakers, flagons and cooking-pots is also present. Pottery of 3rd and 4th century date seems absent, though some of the bead rim dishes could date from the beginning of the 3rd century. The burnished bead rim dishes seem to predominate and when taken with cavetto and square-rimmed cooking pots a closing date of A.D. 180–220 is probable. About 65 samian vessels very largely follow the pattern of the coarse pottery, with Antonine material predominating and the Argonne products being the latest in date. The impression is that this pottery was being discarded in quantity during the second half of the 2nd century and contained some earlier vessels, either as survivals or derived from nearby. In addition, some fragments of vessel and window glass, the largest group of glass found on the site, were found with the pottery. Clearly, there were some glazed windows in the Period I or II houses. It also seems clear that this terrace, at the back of the house, must have been the major domestic rubbish area for several decades!

PERIOD II (Fig. 16)

It is clear that substantial changes were made to the original Period I structure, exclusively on the west side of the building. These involved the construction of a new external west wall to the house, the creation of a small room (Room 7) in the enlarged West Corridor and the addition of a large new room (Room 15) at the south-west corner. These substantial alterations are regarded as Period II and enlarged the house to about 375 sq.m.

West Corridor

The new external west wall (see above) involved the removal of the Period I external corridor wall and its replacement was somewhat poorer in construction. The new wall lay about 40 cm. outside the original wall and increased the corridor's internal width to about 3.00 m.

It is difficult to regard the new outer wall as a calculated improvement, for it only marginally increased the width of the corridor. This seems a very small gain for what was a total re-build of the west side of the building. A much more likely reason is that the Period I west wall was in a bad structural state and it alone had to be replaced. Whilst this may seem an unlikely circumstance the Period I west wall was in fact thinner than the walls of the main rooms. In addition, it had no internal divisions to support it over its length of 30 m. Another factor is that it was flanked by a steep, uphill slope where storm-water and prevailing westerly winds could have caused structural damage. Whatever the precise circumstances, the wall was removed completely and replaced by a new mortared wall 40–50 cm. further uphill with deeper foundations and incorporating some chalk blocks.

As part of these new arrangements the enlarged corridor was provided with a new floor of *opus signinum*, generally 4–6 cm. thick and constructed of mortar containing small tile chips. This floor clearly sealed the abandoned Period I rammed chalk foundations on the west side, which could be seen protruding from beneath it in three places. The new floor survived for about 6 m. near the south end of the corridor, under what later became Rooms 8 and 9, but its original extent is not known. Any southward extension would have been removed under the Period V rebuilding and any northwards extension by the driveway cut through it in 1926. At the same time the north end of the corridor had been provided with a clay floor (see above), which also covered the abandoned Period I chalk foundation. The *opus signinum* floor was later cut through (Period III) and two short cross-walls inserted to create Rooms 8 and 9 (see below).

Room 7

As explained (above), the West Corridor was further divided during the Period II work, by an additional cross-wall near its north end. This seems to have created a small room some 3 m. wide, but of unknown length. On the assumption that Room 1 was the same size as Rooms 2–4, as is suggested, then the north end of the building can be estimated. This suggests that Room 7 may have been about 3.20 m. in length and thus have covered an area of about 10 sq. m.

It was clearly provided with a clay floor, which also passed through the doorway in the new wall, joining it with the rest of the corridor. Of special interest in the south-west corner of Room 7 was a roughly circular pit (F85), about 50 cm. in diameter and 14 cm. deep, cut through the clay floor. This contained the complete skeleton of a small sheep/goat that had been carefully tucked into the pit. It is difficult to explain this burial other than a ritual deposit and indeed such occur at many Roman sites. A very similar burial, of a sheep/goat, was found by the writer in an early Roman pit in *Londinium* in 1968 (Ref. 53) and infant-burials in the foundations of Roman military buildings at Reculver in 1963 and later.

Window Opening in Room 7

An examination of the very large section of fallen wall outside Room 7, revealed an original opening surviving largely intact within it. This must represent an external window, rarely found on Roman villa sites, though no glass or metal fittings were found in association.

The opening had started about 1.20 m. above the Period II clay floor with a horizontal sill built of large tile fragments and some flints all mortared solid. The sides of the opening were vertical and survived to a maximum height of 34 cm., but this was not the original top.

The sides had been built with an internal splay so that the external opening of about 29 cm.

increased to at least 45 cm. internally (Plate V). Allowing for damage to the internal face this may originally have been about 50 cm. The external opening was marginally realigned about 7–8 cm. from the external face, which decreased the angle of the splay. The sides of the opening had also been plastered with a thin layer of fine white mortar containing small pebbles. This also created a very small fillet along the bottom edges.

An examination of the wall here suggested that this opening may not have been an original feature, but inserted at a later date. The normal flint coursing had been replaced around the opening by a mixture of flints, chalk and large tile fragments and lumps of re-used white mortar. The wall thickness seems to have been reduced to about 38 cm. at the level of the opening. This insertion could relate to either Period II (a subsequent alteration) or, to Period III.

Room 15 (Plates VI and XII and Fig. 7. S.13)
At the same time as the West Corridor was being rebuilt and new floors laid, a large new room (Room 15) was added at the south-west corner to create a modest extension. The new north wall of this room continued the south wall of the Period I house for a distance of about 2.50 m. Its new west wall, not quite parallel to the main axis of the villa, was about 9.50 m. in overall length. Its new south wall was traced for only 3.00 m. where it had been cut away by later building work. It seems likely that it would have extended as far as the line of the outside wall of the Period IIIB tank which probably respected it. No traces of an east wall survived due to the Periods III–V alterations which drastically affected this area. It seems likely that Room 15, had an internal area of about 8.75 m. by 4.00 m.

The walls of this new room were noticeably thinner than the main walls of the Period I villa, being generally 40–44 cm. in thickness. They were built of coursed chalk and flints set in a buff mortar, broadly similar to the new outer wall of the Period II West Corridor.

It is clear that this room was terraced slightly into the slope on both its south and west sides (Fig. 7. S.13). In both cases it cut earlier soil deposits and the natural yellow sand. Its construction-trench contained three potsherds, a Patch Grove vessel, a flagon and a rough-cast beaker. All probably date from the late-1st or early 2nd-century.

The cut-base of the terrace seems to have served as the floor and this was found to be surfaced with patches of *opus signinum*, perhaps once more extensive. This was covered with a layer of mottled green-brown loam, representing the primary occupation layer (L.28). This contained 29 potsherds and a bronze pin (No. 10). The pottery included six samian sherds, mostly of Antonine date and fragments of sandy ware vessels' of mid-2nd century date. This was mostly sealed by a thin layer of orange-brown clay loam (L.27) representing a floor. This was in turn sealed by a black-brown loam (L.26), a secondary occupation layer, containing charcoal specks and 81 potsherds. These include four sherds of samian, three of which are of Antonine date and including one sherd matching a vessel from the primary occupation layer below. The coarse pottery included sandy ware cooking pots, some with burnished lattice decoration; some grog-tempered wares and one rough-cast beaker. Most of this seems to be of Antonine date and this deposit represents an upper occupation layer. These were sealed by dumps of soil (L.15–23) containing mortar, flints and tile, which also covered the walls and show that this room was then no longer in use. The domestic rubbish scattered about this room resembles kitchen debris and it maybe that this corner room was built and used as the kitchen of the main house. Some nine post-holes or small pits were detected within this room. Two large fragments of window glass here could indicate that this room was glazed.

As regards dating, Period II clearly superseded Period I which is dated on good circumstantial grounds to about A.D. 140–170 (see above). The pottery from Room 15 seems to be mostly Antonine in date and certainly none need be later than A.D. 200. From this it is clear that Room 15 was in use, perhaps as a domestic kitchen, in the later Antonine period and must relate to Period II and thus date from about A.D. 170–200. The room clearly survived the Period III programme, which was partially modelled around it in A.D. 200–225, but it was removed in Period IV (A.D. 225–250), when it was regarded as expendable. Perhaps by then its age and slight form were presenting problems.

PERIOD IIIA (Fig. 16)

It is clear from the structural evidence in the ground that major additions and some internal alterations took place some years after the completion of the Period II building work. This major programme of works doubled the size of the building and substantially changed its character.

In outline a new East Corridor, some 2.90 m. wide, seems to have been built along the east side of the building and largely matched the earlier West Corridor. A new range of three rooms (Rooms 12, 13A and 14A) was also added to the south end of the building, but separated from it by a new passage (Room 11) which linked with the new East Corridor. The new rooms were substantially incomplete due to extensive damage caused by the construction of the deep hypocausts in Period V and by the construction of the driveway in 1926.

The dating evidence for the Period III work is again largely indirect, for the subsequent destruction of most of the Period III rooms by various agencies has removed all trace of evidence relating to the actual construction. There is, however, adequate circumstantial and relative dating evidence to suggest that the major Period III programme of work took place at about A.D. 200–225.

In detail, the Period III work clearly followed the Period I and Period II building, the former dated A.D. 140–170 (see above). It also clearly predated the Period IV alterations for which fairly abundant evidence survived at the south-west corner of the villa. This suggested (see below) that Period IV dates from about A.D. 225–250. Allowing for Period II, sometime later in the second century as seems probable, the Period III programme of work must have taken place sometime about A.D. 200–225. The scale of the Period IV work was anyway not large and could have followed the Period III work at any interval, being largely a replacement of the old Period II corner extension.

A south-east corner room (Room 12) seems to have been about 5 × 3 m. internally. A second, small room (Room 13A) seems to have been about 5 × 1.50 m. and may have served as a passage. A larger room (Room 14A) about 5.10 × 3.40 m. completed the south-west corner. This block filled the rectangle between Room 15 (Period II) and the south end of the original house (Period I). Nothing of the new south wall survived on site, but its line is suggested by two later walls (Period IIIB and Period IV) that are likely to have followed it.

Within the original building the West Corridor was divided near its centre by the addition of two more transverse walls about 1.50 m. apart (Room 8), both clearly butted to the Period II external wall. Their character also shows them to be of different construction from Period II and they also cut through the Period II *opus signinum* floor. The newly created room here is unusually narrow and resembles an access passage from outside and which could have given access to both sides of the corridor. The effect of the insertion of these two walls was to subdivide the West Corridor, apparently to create extra rooms. If so, that on the south side (shown as Rooms 9 and 10) had an internal length of 8.20 m. That on the north side of the new walls would have had an internal length of 14 m., though it is possible that this was originally subdivided by another cross-wall destroyed when the driveway was built.

Room 5 was divided unequally by an inserted cross-wall into two separate rooms. The smaller (Room 5) was then about 3.75 × 2.40 m. and the larger (Room 6) about 3.70 × 3.00 m. The north and south walls of both rooms seem to have been rebuilt.

The new Rooms 5 and 11 were each provided with a tessellated floor and it seems likely that the tessellated floors in Rooms 2, 3 and 4 were laid at the same time. Nothing can be said about the floors in Rooms 12, 13A and 14A, but it is clear that the new East Corridor was also tessellated.

The effect of all these changes was to increase the length of the building to about 37.50 m., the width to about 14.00 m. and the total area (including Room 15) to about 562 sq. m. It increased the number of rooms from six to about 12 or 13. Clearly, this major building programme upgraded the original structure, by then perhaps about 50 years old and provided a new eastern facade, perhaps a pretentious veranda with a pentice roof. The extra rooms, mostly at the south end may reflect an increase in the family size, such as two related families living under the same roof.

Room 6A (Fig. 5. S.3)
This room was created as part of the Period III building programme, when a wall was constructed across Room 5 of the Period I scheme. This divided the original room unequally and caused Room 6A to be about 3.70 × 3.00 m. New south, east and north walls were constructed, but no trace of a west wall was found for it must have been removed in Period V. Nor had any detail survived the Period V alterations when wide channels were cut through the room for the construction of the channelled hypocaust (Room 6B).

Room 8 (Plate VII and Fig. 5. S.5)
This small room occupied part of what had been the original Period I West Corridor. In Period II the west wall had been replaced and an *opus signinum* floor inserted in this part of the corridor. Room 8 was clearly created in Period III when short walls were built across the corridor, cutting through the *opus signinum* floor. The new walls were about 46 cm. wide and built of flints set in cream mortar, of which only three courses survive.

The room so created was 3.05 × 1.50 m. in size. This is unusually small and it may be that it was constructed to form an entrance-passage from outside. Its south wall was about 1.40 m. in length, for it clearly had a door-opening about 1.45 m. wide linking it with Room 9. The detail here was largely removed in 1959 and replaced with modern concrete. It is possible that there was also an opening here into Room 4.

During the major Period V alterations, it seems likely that this room was abandoned along with the rest of the northern half of the building. Certainly its west wall had gone before the roof tiles fell across its foundations and by the end of the fourth century a shaft (F51) was dug through two of its walls, presumably then missing. The floor had been badly worn and all stratification removed by earlier excavations. A coin (Coin No. 3) of A.D. 270–273 had been found on the floor in 1959.

Room 9 (Plates VIII and X and Fig. 5. S.1 and S.5; Fig. 6. S.12 and Fig. 7. S.14)
This room formed part of the West Corridor under the Period I scheme, but became divided during Period III and converted into a stoke-hole during Period V. In plan, in its final form, the room measured 3.85 × 3.00 m. In detail, the Period I rammed chalk foundations were found on both east and west sides, the former 58 cm. and the latter at least 50 cm. wide. The space between these was again about 2.40 m. There was no trace of an original floor and this must have been of trodden soil. During the Period II alterations, the outside west wall was demolished and replaced by a poorly built wall of flint and chalk about 45 cm. wide. This marginally overlapped the abandoned Period I foundations and increased the width of the room to about 3.00 m.

A new floor, of *opus signinum*, (S.14, L.3) was then laid and this sealed the earlier chalk foundations and butted to the new Period II west wall. The floor was mostly 4–6 cm. thick, but its surface was badly worn through later use. It rested on a base of flints (S.14, L.4) set in a pinky-white mortar, mostly 6–8 cm. thick. Only about 2.70 m. of the floor survived and it is not known how large an area of the West Corridor was originally laid in this way. The floor clearly sealed the pre-villa soils (S.13, L.11) and the builders upcast soils (S.13, L.9). Above the floor most of the stratification had been removed by earlier excavation. A thin band of loam (S.5, L.39) had, however, survived on the floor and this was sealed by a substantial rubble and soil layer (S.5, L.37), relating to the final demolition of the house.

What is clear is that during Period III, a pair of cross-walls was inserted across the West Corridor to create a small room (Room 8). One was also the north wall of Room 9 and it was constructed at the same time as the new wall on the east side of the corridor. The construction trench for the new north wall clearly cut away the *opus signinum* floor, whilst the wall itself butted to the Period II west wall and was set at a slight angle to it. The foundation-trench for the new east wall also removed a strip of the Period II floor, some 15–30 cm. wide.

The new north wall was about 46 cm. wide and was built of flints set in cream mortar and survived three courses high. The new east wall was about 60 cm. wide, similarly constructed and survived to a maximum height of three courses. Any south wall for this room would have been removed by the Period V work.

In Period V the south end of Room 9 was cut away to an unknown extent during the construction of Room 10, a hypocausted room cut about 70 cm. below original floor-level. The internal floor area was also cut away to create a D-shaped pit to serve as a stoke-hole for the furnace arch in Room 10. This process also cut away part of the buried Period I foundations on the west side and much of the natural yellow sand. The stoke-hole was about 2.05 × 2.10 m., had steep sides and a flat base. The base contained a single layer of large tile fragments set in mortar, partly burnt, serving as a base for part of the stoke-hole (Plate X). Beneath this tiled base was a deposit of mottled soils (L.2), about 10–15 cm. deep, which seems to be the bottom fill of the stoke-hole as dug. The stoke-hole and most of Room 9 had been cleared during the excavation in 1927. The only finds associated with this room were some 24 sherds found on the surface of the *opus signinum* floor. These include Patch Grove ware, sandy ware cooking pots and a possible indented beaker. The pottery is probably late-2nd century and may have been discarded during Period II.

Room 11 (Plate XI and Fig. 5. S3 and Fig. 7. S.15)

This room seems to have served as an east-west passageway linking the major elements of the house (Periods III–V). It flanked the south end of the original building (Period I) and linked the north end of Room 15 (Period II) with the newly created East Corridor (also Period III). It also flanked new Rooms 13A and 14A where there were probably linking doorways. It had also been badly damaged by the driveway made in 1926.

The 1988 excavation established that there was no east wall and that it shared a floor in common with the East Corridor. The north wall was also rebuilt under the Period III scheme and served Rooms 5 and 6 (see above). Similarly, the south wall also served new Rooms 13A and 14A. Its west wall must have been the Period II east wall of Room 15, now gone. The overall length surviving was about 7.00 m. and its width varied from about 2.20–2.40 m. This variation seems to have been caused by the pre-existing minor misalignment of Room 15 (Period II) when it was added to the end of the original building (Period I). Its original length was probably 8.00–8.50 m., but its west end had been cut away in Period V when Room 16 was constructed.

It is clear that Room 11 had been provided with a substantial floor, surfaced with plain red tesserae. Some 700 survived in 1988, covering an area of about 2.20 × 0.35 m. The 1927 plan shows many more and it is clear that the driveway must have removed a large section of floor in addition to these. In detail, the base of the floor (S.15. L.5) consisted of flints in loose cream mortar, mostly 5–15 cm. thick. This was capped by a layer (S.15. L.4) of cream mortar containing many pebbles and occasional tile chips, some 8 cm. deep at the west end, but increasing to 15 cm. towards the east where it offset the slope of the ground to help create a level surface. On top of this was a thin white mortar (S15. L.3) with tile chips, 1–3 cm. thick, serving as the bedding layer for the tesserae. At the extreme west end of the surviving floor, was a small patch of 25 tesserae set marginally lower and in a cream-pink mortar. This may represent a later repair. No stratified deposits or objects were recovered from above this floor and its relationship with the north wall had been destroyed by a trench dug in 1927.

This room sealed the pre-villa deposits (S.15. L.10) and features (F101, F103 and F104). The substantial foundation for the Period III floor also sealed a thin band (S.15. L.8) of white mortar and patches of red *opus signinum*, both perhaps forming part of the external construction levels relating to Periods I and II.

The inside face of the Period III north wall had a thin strip of white mortar rendering near its west end. This started below finished floor-level and may indicate how the whole wall was finished.

Room 12

This new room (Period III) occupied the extreme south-east corner of the new south range. Very little indeed had survived the construction of the two driveways in 1926 where formation levels were cut even deeper than the Roman foundations. A section of the north-east corner of the room was plotted approximately by Elliston Erwood, but this was subsequently destroyed.

The 1988 excavation picked up the lower foundations of the north-west corner of the room. These took the form of medium-sized flints laid, unmortared, in foundation-trenches generally 60 cm. in width and originally perhaps 30 cm. deep. The west foundations had been cut through when the hypocaust was inserted during the Period V reconstruction when this room became part of the extended Room 13B. No trace of any wall survived in 1988, nor any associated stratified deposits or finds.

It is possible to reposition the corner recorded in 1927 to line up with the surviving outer wall of the East Corridor found in 1988. This shows the east-west width of Room 12 at about 3 m. On the assumption that its south wall followed the line of the surviving south wall of Room 14D, which is the most likely arrangement, then it is possible to calculate the internal length of this room at about 5.00 m. Hence, this corner room had an internal area of only about 15 sq. m.

Room 13A

This new room occupied a small area between Rooms 12 and 14A in the added south range (Period III). Again, very little had survived the construction of the 1926 driveway, nor the construction of the deep hypocaust for Room 13B in Period V.

The 1988 excavation picked up the north end of the room and the stubs of the east and west walls, but only at foundation-level. Again these took the form of unmortared flints set in a trench 60–80 cm. wide and about 20 cm. deep. The west foundation cut deeper than the other two and it is possible that another building phase is represented. So little survived that it is impossible to be certain. No stratified deposits or finds were found associated with this room.

On the evidence of the foundations it is likely that this room had an east–west internal width of about 1.70 m. Again on the assumption of a common south wall the internal length can be calculated at about 5.00 m. Hence, this room was only some 7.50 sq. m. in area, just half the size of Room 12. It could in fact have been a passageway linking the Room 11 passage with the outside area south of the villa.

A small section of the west foundation was found under the hypocaust channel of Room 13B where it was 80 cm. wide. An irregular mass of flint, chalk and ginger mortar at the south end may have related in some way but the exact relationship could not be determined.

Room 14A (Fig. 6. S.9)
This room was the largest of the three new rooms in the added south range (Period III) and was probably the principal room of the range. Again much had been removed by the insertion of the hypocaust in Period V, by the 1926 driveway and by the widening of Crofton Road some years later.

The 1988 excavation picked up clear evidence of the north and east walls, but only slight traces of the south and west walls. The extant walls had only survived about two courses high and this showed them to have been built of flints set in ginger mortar. The north wall was mostly 75 cm. thick and rested on an unmortared foundation of rolled flints some 50 cm. deep. The east wall had similar foundations, generally 60–86 cm. wide. No stratified deposits or finds were found in association with this room, due to the later damage.

On the evidence of the little which survives of the south and west walls it is possible to suggest that this room had been about 4.70 × 3.60 m. This, however, is less than the suggested width of the new south block but the area beyond has been destroyed.

Isolated sections of the substantial floor (L.18–19) of this room were located near its centre, buried beneath the later masonry. This had a base of large flints up to 30 cm. thick covered by a white mortar floor 12 cm. deep. This is unusually massive and must have been constructed to take a substantial weight. In addition, its surface was at least 30 cm. lower than an adjacent floor (Room 11). These fundamental structural factors suggest that this room may have served as a tank, or bath and was designed to hold water. Significantly, perhaps, this room was superseded by a slightly smaller room (Room 14B of Period IIIB), almost certainly built to contain water in the form of a tank, or bath (see below).

The East Corridor (Fig. 5. S.4 and Fig. 7)
This corridor seems to have flanked the east side of the building, largely matching the original (Period I) corridor on the west side. About half its probable length had been removed by the railway cutting, totally unrecorded, with most of the rest having been removed when the driveways were cut in 1926. A T-shaped section of the masonry, recorded in 1927 but then destroyed provides evidence for its south end and this is shown on the plans (Fig. 16) in its corrected position. This corridor linked with the passage (Room 11) and may have provided access to each of the main rooms, or at least some of them. It is likely that it also allowed access from the new corner room (Room 12). Its width must have been about 2.90 m. and its length about 30 m.

The only section of this corridor found in 1988 was at the edge of the railway cutting where a short piece of masonry and a small area of possible floor survived. The wall had a massive foundation of chalk, flints and mortar totalling 80 cm. in depth and 85 cm. wide. It was substantially different from the rammed chalk foundations of Period I. The wall itself was built of flint set in a white gritty mortar and only survived one course high. Only some 2.75 m. of its length remained. The internal area showed that above the pre-villa soils all that survived was a thin layer of white mortar 2 cm. thick. The 1927 plan shows a substantial area at the south end of this corridor as tessellated. No trace of this remained in 1988.

The south end of the surviving masonry appears to have been cut through by a large ovoid pit (F62), which measured 3.06 × 2.15 m. with steep sides and a cupped base. Its filling consisted of various soil deposits containing a mid-1st century brooch (No. 3), 28 sherds (Nos. 62 and 102) including six samian vessels of Flavian to Antonine date. The coarse pottery includes two colour-coated vessels of late-3rd or 4th century date. Most of the pit had been excavated in 1956 and the surviving stratification is unsatisfactory. On balance it seems likely that the pit was dug through the wall sometime in the 4th century.

A small irregular patch of worn white mortar containing pebbles, some 1–3 cm. thick, was found outside the East Corridor wall and cut by Pit F62. This extended about 1.30 m. from the wall and had a maximum width of about 85 cm. On its surface was a disturbed group of about 20 plain red tesserae.

On its merits this represents a small section of a thin floor of another room, but its position *outside* the building makes this unlikely. It may be significant that it lay close to the centre of the villa, following the suggested Period III arrangements. It is possible that a central entrance had existed here and, if so, a small external porch may also have existed. The thin floor with its tessellation would then have been inside such a structure. Whilst this could explain the presence of this feature here it must be said that there is no other evidence of a porch or external room. The railway cutting will have removed all other traces.

PERIOD IIIB (Fig. 6. S.11)

Room 14B (Tank or Bath)

At some stage subsequent to the construction of Period IIIA, a single new room appears to have been inserted into the south range over Room 14A. This (Room 14B) was somewhat smaller in size, but as the walls had been planed off to floor-level by later alterations, the precise size is not known. Only the north-west corner and part of the south-east corner remained intact. This showed the walls to be built of flint and tile set in white mortar with small pebbles and varying from 56–74 cm. in thickness. From what survives it is clear that the north–south internal width was about 2.50 m. and the east-west internal width between 2.75–2.90 m.

Of specific interest was an internal vertical lining, surviving on parts of the north, west and south walls. This took the form of a red-pink *opus signinum*, some 2–3 cm. thick, but surviving to a maximum height of only 5 cm. at one point. The corresponding floor, which seemed to rest against the lining, was of a hard white mortar. It was about 10 cm. thick and it rested on a foundation of flints set in white mortar another 12 cm. deep. This substantial floor also sat directly over the equally substantial floor of Room 14A, thus giving a massive total depth of about 60 cm.

About 60 cm. along the north wall, from the north-west corner, was the outline of a small projection into the room, built against the vertical lining. This was 30 cm. wide and had been greater than 30 cm. in length. A tile which formed the base of this projection had been robbed away, but the outline was again preserved by another vertical *opus signinum* lining. On its merits this small room, with its unique lining on this site and substantial floor, resembles a shallow tank for holding water. A shallow bath seems possible, but no trace of corresponding drains, water inlets or outlets, were found. However, the adjacent area to the south had been badly disturbed and this must remain inconclusive. Significantly, perhaps, it replaced Room 14A which may also have been a tank, or bath.

PERIOD IV (Plate XII and Fig. 6. S.10 and Fig. 16)

Sometime after the completion of the Period III rebuilding, an alteration took place at the south-west corner of the villa. The old projecting, slightly-built Room 15 of the Period II villa was completely removed and replaced by a new room (Room 14C), in a substantially different position. The effect of this was to abandon the early extension. Instead, the new west wall was built on the line of the surviving Period II West Corridor, though marginally misaligned. The new building work probably took place about A.D. 225–250 (see below).

Room 14C
In detail the new wall was constructed in a shallow terrace (the Middle Terrace on the plan), which partly removed the dumps, floors and walls of Room 15 (Fig. 16). The new wall did not, however, have a deep foundation and its base rested upon the lower occupation soils surviving from Room 15. Indeed, part of the original patchy *opus signinum* floor of the earlier room survived inside the new Period IV walls. The new west wall had a total length of 6.60 m., was 60 cm. wide and was constructed of flints set in a cream-buff mortar with pebbles. Its south-west corner was quoined with flat bricks and the new south wall survived for a distance of about 2.60 m. A corresponding north wall survived for a distance of 1.50 m. and seemed to be marginally greater in width. It seems that the west wall of Room 14B must have been removed as part of the new arrangements. This would have created a new room (Room 14C) about 5.50 m. by perhaps about 5.00 m., if the east wall of the earlier room was retained. Although this seems likely, it cannot now be proved due to subsequent damage. This rebuilding work marginally reduced the overall area of the villa to about 540 sq. m.

Exactly how the space between this new Room 14C and the south end of the West Corridor was treated is not clear, due to the insertion here of Room 16 in Period V. It is clear that part of the demolished Room 15 had occupied this space during Periods II and III. The most likely explanation is that the passageway (Room 11) was extended to the west side of the building.

A small section of wall-plaster was found adhering to a narrow block of soil on the inside face of the south wall of this new room and this survived to a height of 15 cm. (Fig. 6. S.10). It was painted pink-white with red splashes and this probably represents a dado. It was not associated with a solid floor, but rested on dumped layers of mottled clay-loam (L.10–12). These had later been substantially cut away when the hypocaust of Period V had been inserted.

The Middle Terrace (Period IV)
A well-defined cut through the soils filling Room 15 (Period II) represents a narrow terrace into the ground at the south-west end of the Roman house. Its position corresponds closely with the size of Room 14C (Period IV) and its seems clear that it was cut at the same time, to facilitate its construction. It was about 6.80 m. in length, about 1.45 m. in width, but extending under the walls and was 43 cm. deep. It had a sloping side and a flat base.

It had been filled with soil in stages, mostly grey and brown clay loams. These contained a substantial mixture of fragmented mortar, *opus signinum*, chalk, flint and tiles mostly representing decayed or demolished structures. It also included 32 plain tesserae.

Some seven deposits here contained about 200 pieces of pottery. The majority seems to date from the later-2nd century, or early-3rd century and includes the standard cooking pots and dishes and a mortarium (No. 71). The samian is Hadrian-Antonine or Antonine in date. However, several colour-coated vessels and flanged dishes (Nos. 103–106), must mostly date from the late-3rd century. On the pottery evidence, allowing for some of the earlier pottery having been derived from the slope above, it seems clear that this terrace was filled progressively during the second half of the third century. This in turn suggests that the Period IV work probably took place no later than about A.D. 250.

The more critical dating evidence for Period IV mainly comes from soils dumped on top of the demolished Room 15 walls. These soils were generally 30–35 cm. thick and had been cut by the Middle Terrace, created for the construction of the Period IV walls. Here nine deposits contained about 650 fragments of pottery (Nos. 95–101) including 33 sherds of samian ware (No. 40). Although some mid-2nd century material is included the majority seems to date from about A.D. 180–225. This includes several shallow dishes with either plain lips, bead rims or, occasionally, flanged rims. Several cooking pots have cavetto or squared rims. The latest vessels are unlikely to be later in date-range than A.D. 250. These layers also contained several small finds including a ring (No. 2), a bronze bracelet (No. 5), bone pins (Nos. 17–18) and glass vessels (Nos. 37–38).

A small amount of dating evidence was also found in the very limited deposits relating to Period IV, which had survived the extensive rebuilding of Period V. Some 11 sherds included a samian Form 33 of Antonine date and coarse pottery dating up to about A.D. 200 were recovered from the soil sealed by the slight mortar floor and seems to represent derived material. At least these indicate that the floor could not have been laid before A.D. 200. In addition the *in situ* wall-plaster sealed a sherd of samian, a Form 31 of Antonine date, again providing a *terminus post quem*.

The combined dating evidence, therefore, strongly suggests that Phase IV must date from after A.D. 200. Indeed the pottery in the dumps sealing Room 15 and into which the Period IV terrace was cut, even suggests a date after A.D. 225. The terrace was itself being filled in the second half of the 3rd century, so a construction date of A.D. 225–250 seems the most likely.

Further evidence for the final filling of the Middle Terrace comes from 3 coins (Coin Nos. 2, 4 and 22) of Gallienus (A.D. 260–8), Barbarous Radiate (A.D. 270–290) and a corroded 3rd or 4th century type. These had been dropped, probably at the same time, on a soil surface which extended over the filled Period IV terrace. They suggest that the terrace was filled no later than about A.D. 300 and may have been dropped by the Period V occupants, or even its builders!

PERIOD V (Plates XIII–XIV and Fig. 16)
It is clear from the relative structural disposition of the masonry, that the final major programme of building was carried out at the south end of the Roman house. This was done sometime after the construction of Room 14C (Period IV) and almost certainly in the latter part of the 3rd century. This work very substantially changed the character of the building and reduced its size to less than half of the Period III house. It seems to reflect changes in the needs of the occupants, perhaps even a new family moving to the site.

The new building work saw the construction of a suite of five rooms (Rooms 6B, 10, 13B, 14D and 16) at the south end, all provided with elaborate hypocaust heating-systems otherwise absent in the house. The construction of this underfloor heating required deep excavation and the removal of many of the earlier walls and floors. In addition, Room 9 was converted into a stoke-hole and a large area of its floor removed to facilitate low-level firing of Room 10. Here the heat passed through a diagonal arch into Room 10 before being drawn through two openings into Room 6B and through another arched opening into Room 16.

The heating from these three rooms did not reach Rooms 13B and 14D which must have had their own arrangements. No additional stoke-hole was found, but with three corners of Room 14D solid, it could only have been adjacent to the south-east channel in the area subsequently destroyed. Indeed, it seems highly likely that a single furnace here fed both Rooms 13B and 14D.

An examination of the plan shows how the rebuilding work swept away the southern end of the West Corridor and replaced it with Rooms 10 and 16. It converted Room 6 into a heated room, but seems to have left Room 11 (the tessellated passage), substantially intact.

The Period IV walls of Room 14C were retained on the south, west and north sides, but a major new east wall was inserted to be shared with Room 13B. The latter replaced whatever then survived of Period III at that point. Significantly, the new west wall of Rooms 10 and 16 was aligned on the Period IV west wall and not on the earlier West Corridor.

It is also clear that the northern half of the Roman House was then abandoned. Room 9, cut through to create a stoke-hole, was almost certainly the limit of what was retained for the west wall of Room 8 was soon removed. Tiles from the adjacent roof had fallen over its exposed foundations and also slid off much of the rest of the roof on this side. A major section of actual wall, still 11 courses high and containing a window-opening, had fallen onto these tiles at the north end. The adjacent section of the corridor had never been used again and was being buried by an extensive dump in the late-3rd century. A shaft (F58) had been cut through the collapsed tile and masonry outside Room 7. In addition, another large Roman shaft (F51, see below) was cut through the foundations and tile collapse in Room 8. Both shafts were probably dug and filled in the late-4th century when much of the northern part of the building had been demolished. It seems likely that much of the masonry here was robbed to help the extensive Period V building work and perhaps later for minor repairs. The shortened Period V building seems to have been about 20 × 14 m., if both Rooms 9 and 4 are included, giving a total area of about 280 sq. m.

The Period V building work also seems to have included the cutting of a new terrace (the Late Terrace, see below), generally 1–3 m. wide on the west side of the building and ending by Room 8. This contained pottery of late-3rd century date. The Period V building was also provided with a flanking ditch (F1), some 2.50 m. wide and about 6 m. from the villa on the uphill side. This must have collected storm-water from the hill above. It flowed marginally to the north and contained largely 4th century material.

Details of each room are given below.

Room 6B (Plate XV and Fig. 5. S.3)

This room had clearly been converted during Period V when the suite of five hypocausted rooms had been inserted. Room 6B lay next to the principal room (Room 10) which was in turn next to the stoke-hole and maximum point of heat. Hence the hot air from the furnace had to pass across Room 10 to reach Room 6, by means of two openings in the common wall. From here the hot air passed along two east–west channels the length of the room to the north-east and south-east corners where there must have been vertical flues.

In detail, the openings in the west wall were about 45 cm. in width and survived to heights of 28 cm. and 52 cm. They were constructed predominantly of complete tegulae roof tiles and some flint bonded in white mortar. Those on the north opening, where at least nine complete tiles were used, were about 45 cm. in length and 32 cm. wide tapering down to about 26 cm. at the lower edge. These tiles were laid horizontally to a height of about 34 cm. above the base of the opening where they stepped out to form the start of a corbelled arch that would have been at least 52 cm. high. The opening on the south side was too damaged to provide additional details.

The two channels were substantially built, each constructed in a wide sloping cut against the pre-existing Period III north and south walls. The cuts about 1.25–1.50 m., as surviving, must have removed about two-thirds of the Period III floor and had a depth of about 70 cm., when originally cut.

Into these cuts were built two open channels, both about 47 cm. wide and surviving to about 40 cm. in height. Each channel was lined by side walls, mostly of coursed flints and some tile set in buff mortar 20–33 cm. in width. Each wall contained a single course of tiles, some broken including tegulae and presumably reused from elsewhere on the site. The ends of the channels butted to the east wall. The base of the channels consisted of cream mortar and pebbles (not removed).

The channels had been truncated prior to 1988, but would certainly have been about 50 cm. high. Hence no trace of any bridging tiles survived, but on the south side two distinctive slots were found in the external wall framing the channel. These were about 15–24 cm. wide and about 45 cm. deep clearly cut into the face of the Period III wall. Their largely symmetrical spacing strongly suggests that they were the rebates for the base of vertical wall-flues. Allowing for end flues this suggests that Room 6B originally had six vertical wall-flues in all, two in each wall and two at the east end.

As regards dating evidence, the north channel contained no finds as it had been cleaned out in 1927. The south channel (Fig. 8) contained only 13 sherds, including a colour-coated bottle, a flanged dish and the rim of a colour-coated bowl. These seem to date from the later-3rd or early-4th centuries and were presumably redeposited there following later robbing.

Room 10 (Plates XVI, XVII and XVIII and Fig. 5. S.5. Fig. 6. S.7. S.12)

This important room is situated on the west side of the villa and occupies what had been part of the south end of the West Corridor of the Period I building. It was constructed as part of the major Period V rebuilding programme with a deep underfloor hypocaust which totally removed all trace of earlier walls, floor and pre-villa deposits. It had been largely emptied during the 1927 excavation, but about ten pilae are shown *in situ* on the surviving plan. An apse shown on that plan did not exist, the suggested evidence for it being one of the support walls just seen in Room 16 (see below). Photographs survive of the excavation of this room in 1927.

In Period V new walls were built on all four sides and clearly the external Period II wall was regarded as too shallow and poorly built. All the walls were constructed of neatly coursed flints and occasional tiles set in a hard white-buff mortar. The south, west and north walls were all clearly more substantial and 65–68 cm. wide at the base. At about 55 cm. above the base level the walls were reduced in width to about 58 cm. to create an internal offset on three sides, mostly 4–7 cm. wide. The offsets themselves were formed by one or more tiles and it is likely that these supported the edges of the bridging tiles capping the hypocausts. Parts of the lower walls had been rendered. The east wall, shared internally with Room 6, was only about 50 cm. wide and had no obvious offset.

The four walls survive to varying maximum heights. The north wall was 91 cm. high (8 courses). The west wall was 1.01 m. high (12 courses). The south wall was 81 cm. high (8 courses) and the east wall only 62 cm. high (8 courses). These walls enclosed an area 3.67 × 3.15 m. at base-level, but with the wall reduction above the offset the actual room size would have been increased to about 3.81 × 3.22 m., about 11.50 sq. m.

The major element of the room was clearly a substantial underfloor hypocaust contained in the lower part of this deep room. It took the form of a pillared system, whereby stacks of flat tiles supported a solid floor, a method commonly used in many Roman buildings. Only the bases of six stacks survived (see plan), mostly at the north-west where three and four tiles bonded with brown clay remained in two vertical positions (Fig. 6. S.7). These tiles were generally 21 × 21 × 3 cm. in size and of a hard sandy red fabric. The spacing, centre to centre, of the three adjacent stacks on the west side was about 55–60 cm. This fairly standard spacing would require 30 stacks of tiles to fill the available space in this room. Each stack, allowing for the bonding layer between each tile, seems to have had about 14 tiles which produces a total of 420 for the whole room. Each stack would have been about 55 cm. high to correspond with the offset on the adjacent walls.

It seems certain from well-known systems elsewhere, that the tile-stacks (pilae) would have been capped by large bridging tiles forming a solid bed across the room. No trace of these survived *in situ*, but small fragments of certain bridging tiles were found on the site. These are normally a standard size, often 54 × 54 × 5 cm. A bed of these, laid 6 × 7 would fit almost exactly across the room requiring 42 tiles in all. It seems clear that a substantial concrete floor would have been laid on this, perhaps up to 10–12 cm. thick to bring it up to the surviving floor-level in the nearly passageway (Room 11). The stacks were based on a floor of cream mortar and pebble, some 5–6 cm. in depth which covered the whole room and extended through the wall openings into Rooms 6 and 16. In 1988, although variably worn, these floors were found to be level within a tolerance of about 3 cm.

The hypocaust in Room 10 was supplied with hot air from a fire in the stoke-hole in Room 9, through a large tiled arch in the common (north) wall. This arch survived partly intact in 1927, but its top was subsequently damaged. Its base was constructed of flints, where it was about 40 cm. in width. The sides were built of six courses of large flat tiles, upon which sprang an arch. Only the lower four courses survive, but it seems that originally the arch may have contained 14 tiles in all. The surviving tiles had been badly cracked through intense heat.

What is significant is that this arch was not placed centrally in the north wall of Room 10, but set about a third of the way from the north-west corner. Equally significant is the fact that the arched opening was set at a marked angle to the wall in the direction of the south-east corner of the room. Fragments of three tiles on the adjacent floor suggest a small diagonal wall, perhaps acting as a heat deflector.

These unusual variations may be explained by the fact that the stoke-hole also fed the hypocausts in the adjacent Rooms 6B and 16. Whereas Room 16 was aligned directly on Room 10, the other (Room 6B) was built to the east. It seems clear that this angled flue-arch was a compromise to supply both rooms equally from a single source.

The corresponding opening (Fig. 8) in the south wall of Room 10 was 38 cm. wide at the base, built centrally, but slightly at an angle. This opening was built of flat tiles, of which eight courses survive, but there was no suggestion of a curved arch. The tile courses projected slightly outwards so that the opening was reduced to about 25 cm. at the seventh course. This is clearly the general form of a corbelled arch and it seems likely that the opening was closed over at a height of about 55 cm. to correspond with the bridging tiles in both rooms.

On the east side were two openings which provided heat for the channels in Room 6B. These were 44 and 47 cm. wide at the base, constructed of flints and tiles, reducing marginally to widths of 33 and 45 cm., respectively. No trace of curved arches were found and these openings were probably matching corbelled arches, similar to that in the south wall. That on the north side survived 52 cm. in height and that on the south side only 28 cm. high.

The hot air clearly circulated beneath the floor of Room 10 and then up inside the walls by means of vertical flues. Traces of these were found set in the faces of the south, west and north walls. One was found in the north wall, two were placed symmetrically in the south wall and two survived in the larger west wall. The latter wall probably originally had a total of four, allowing for later damage, perhaps spaced at intervals of about 1.05 m. The flue openings were normally about 20 × 20 cm. in section as set in the walls. These started about 20–25 cm. above the base and thus about 30–35 cm. below the implied level of the capping bridging tiles. Fragments of only three box-flue tiles survived *in situ*, but these prove that they were inserted just below floor-level. In detail, these box-flue tiles were about 10 × 16 cm. in section, had a circular hole on two opposite sides about 21 cm. from one end and thus probably had a total length of about 42 cm.

The dating evidence for Room 10 is very limited, for clearly the actual floor and most of the hypocaust had been robbed out. The various layers (S.5, L. 9–13 and 29–34) above clearly formed as part of the post-demolition process and even these had been substantially truncated by the 1927 excavation. Only some 29 sherds of pottery were found on the base of the hypocaust, mostly a colour-coated bottle (No. 107) of late-3rd century date. The other sherds include a grit-tempered beaker of probable 4th century date (No. 108).

Room 16 (Plate XIX and Fig. 5. S.5 and Fig. 6. S.6)
This small room occupied what would have been the south end of the West Corridor of the Period I scheme. Its construction in Period V, as a deeply cut hypocaust room, removed all traces of any structural evidence relating to the earlier periods. Internally, it measured 3.35 × 2.70 m., butting to a Period IV wall on the south side, but including new walls on the north and west sides. No new wall was found on the east side where it seems likely there was a wide opening, giving access to the passage on that side (Room 11). The new walls on the west and north sides were 55 cm. and 60 cm. wide, respectively. These walls consisted of neatly coursed flint set in an off-white mortar. In detail the west wall survived 1.12 m. high (ten courses) and the north wall 81 cm. high (eight courses), the latter provided with a large flue arch (see above).

The hypocaust had been constructed within this room, but unusually including low dwarf walls on all four sides. These were mostly 30–37 cm. wide, had survived to a height of 38–50 cm. and were intended to provide ledges for the outside edges of the bridging-tiles. A pillared form of hypocaust had been built within this reduced area, though only a single tile of the south-west stack survived *in situ*. Its position strongly suggests that a total of 12 evenly spaced stacks would originally have existed. This spacing would have supported a bed of large bridging tiles, each about 54 × 54 × 5 cm. in size with their corners resting on the columns and the ledges, as required. A total of 20 bridging tiles would have been required to complete this floor!

In detail, the surviving pila tile was about 21 × 21 × 3 cm. and it is likely that each stack contained about 14 tiles, hence some 168 in all. With bonding between each tile the total height would have been about 55 cm. (as in Room 10), upon which would have been the standard bridging tile (5 cm.) and on this a concrete floor (perhaps 10–12 cm.). Together, this would have created a floor about 70 cm. above the hypocaust base and thus match very closely the surviving floor-levels in the linking passageway (Room 11) and in Room 10. The hot air from the arched opening in the north wall would have circulated beneath such a suspended floor in the normal way.

The dwarf walls were built of flint and some tile set in an off-white mortar containing small pebbles. They were rendered on their vertical faces. The two support walls on the north and west sides were built as an integral part of the main walls. That on the south side butted to pre-existing Period III and Period IV walls which by their variable thickness, caused the dwarf wall to taper at one end. Any earlier east wall must have been removed when the room was built and the new dwarf wall then inserted.

The dwarf walls had not been constructed across the corners of the rooms, but had been angled back to leave narrow channels at each. These channels were generally 50–60 cm. in length, 20–30 cm. in width and the full height of the dwarf walls (Fig. 8). They were certainly provided to allow hot air to circulate from the underfloor area up inside the walls at each corner where a vertical flue must have been provided. These had been totally robbed out when the floor and superstructure were removed. The single pila to survive rested on a pad of light brown mortar. The base of the hypocaust was formed by a 3 cm. layer of cream mortar containing pebbles, a form of concrete, of which about half the area had survived.

As regards dating, the lower fill of the hypocaust contained 12 potsherds. These included a mixture of fabrics, but probably mostly of late-3rd or 4th century date, including a sherd of possible Farnham Ware. The demolition layer covering the walls contained another 26 small potsherds of several fabrics. These include a colour-coated vessel, a dish with a concave side and a flanged bowl (No. 109). These last seem to date from the late-3rd or 4th centuries and presumably washed in during the post-Roman silting of the site. A cluster of five tesserae on the base of the room are likely to have fallen in from Room 11. As with Room 10, the soil deposits (S.5, L. 16–18 and 21–27 and S.6, L. 8–20) in this room had all formed at different times after the hypocaust had been robbed and clearly relate to the final phases of the site.

Room 13B (Plates XX and XXI and Fig. 6, S.8)

This room occupied the south-east corner of the Roman house and it was clearly the largest room in the whole history of the building. It was created as part of the Period V rebuilding programme and its construction removed earlier Rooms 12, 13A and the eastern side of Room 14A. Its southern side was removed when Crofton Road was widened and its eastern side destroyed when the driveways were built in 1926. Nearly half the original room had survived and this was first found in 1988.

In detail, the west wall of this room was newly constructed and shared with Room 14D (see below). No other wall survived, but the lines of the other three can be clearly suggested by projecting extant walls. This suggests that the original room had been about 5.55 × 8 m. internally, or about 44 sq. m.

The room had been provided with a substantial underfloor hypocaust, similar to that in Room 14D and almost certainly built at the same time. This, too, was a chanelled system and although the precise layout was different the same method of construction seems to have been used. Initially, a large hole had been dug through most of the centre of the room, leaving intact blocks of soil and masonry about 50 cm. wide on at least the west and north sides. If this same arrangement applied to the east and south sides then the cut would have been about 4 × 7 m. in extent. The exposed faces had been revetted with tile fragments placed vertically. The base was lined with a thin layer of pink-white mortar and pebbles and the channels and separating blocks built on that.

It seems that about half of the hypocaust survived in part, entirely in the western part of the room. From this it is possible to sketch in the likely arrangement for the rest of the room. This shows four main blocks built of chalk blocks set in brown clay, with a single occasional tile course. Parts of three of these blocks have survived, but only one size is known and this measures 1.75 × 1.26 m. The four solid blocks were separated by channels mostly 26–30 cm. wide and not less than 48 cm. high.

The blocks were in turn enclosed by similar channels, 27–55 cm. wide and also at least 47 cm. high. These were joined at each corner by a diagonal channel leading to the corners of the room. Only one such radiating channel had survived 2.00 m. in length, 20–35 cm. wide and partly cut through surviving masonry. No doubt vertical flues had been constructed above those in the wall corners. The sides of the outer channels were strongly built of chalk blocks set in clay, with some tile, mostly 40 cm. wide. The voids behind these walls had been filled with soil and some rubble to consolidate the structure. No doubt a layer of large bricks had been placed over the channels (as in Room 14D) and a mortar floor laid overall. No trace of these survived anywhere in Room 13B.

As regards dating evidence, six potsherds were recovered from the actual structure of the channels. Clearly, the hypocaust was constructed later than the manufacture of the pottery, which includes a late-2nd century dish and cooking pot. On this evidence the hypocaust must have been constructed sometime after A.D. 200. A fragment of a glass bottle (No. 36) was also found here.

The fill of the hypocaust channels (L.15-18) was mostly brown loam or clay with charcoal specks at the base. These contained fourteen potsherds which probably collected there after

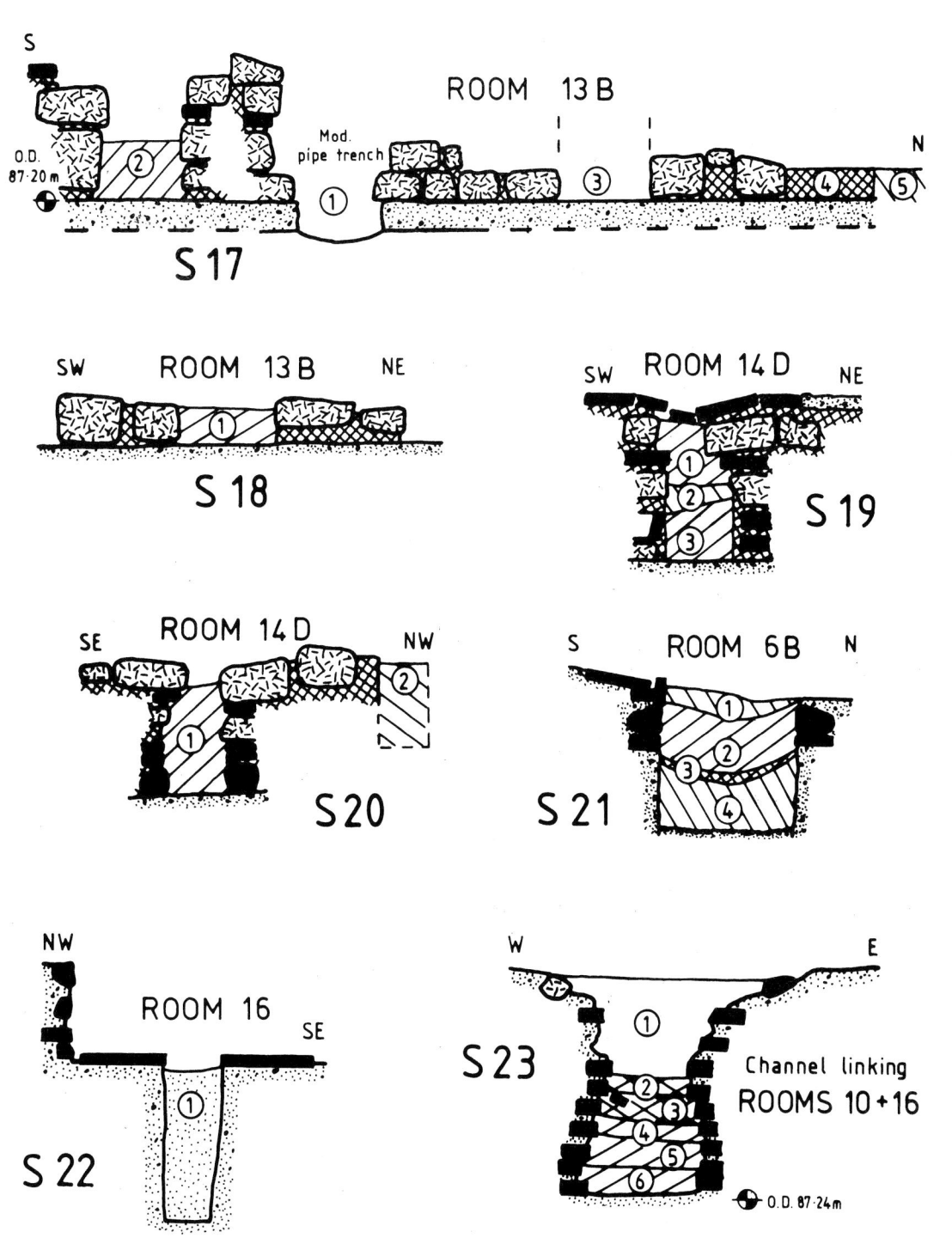

Fig. 8. Sections across hypocaust channels, various rooms (1/20)

the hypocaust went out of use. It includes two straight-sided dishes (No. 110) and a flanged bowl which are of late-3rd or 4th century date. It seems probable that the hypocaust went out of use during the later-4th century and may even have been robbed by that time. Part of a shale bracelet (No. 27) was also found with the pottery.

Room 14D (Plates XXII–XXIV and Fig. 6, S.8. 9. 10. 11)
This large room occupied the south-west corner of the Roman house during Period V and is the most substantial and impressive room surviving on the site. It was not revealed by the earlier excavations, but the south-east corner was destroyed when Crofton Road was widened.

This room formed part of the major Period V conversion of the south end of the villa when a suite of five hypocausted rooms was inserted. This room (14D) superseded the existing room (14C) of Period IV, but utilized the Period IV walls on the south, west and north sides. A new wall was built on the east side where it cut through all pre-existing walls and floors at that point. The room then measured 5.40 m. north–south, by 4.52 m. east–west and covered an area of about 25 sq. m. The new wall on the east side was 65 cm. wide and built of buff coloured mortar containing chalk specks. Its foundation survived at least 65 cm. high though the superstructure had been cut away.

The hypocaust had been carefully constructed, but not with fine precision which anyway may not have been needed. The first operation was to cut a rectangular hole, 4.20 × 3.45 m., through the centre of the room to a depth of about 50 cm. This also destroyed all the earlier walls and floors in this central area. This large excavation left a substantial block of stratified soil (S.8. L.21–26) and structural elements on each side of the room which had the effect of supporting the earlier walls which were much shallower than the hypocaust. This is likely to have been a planned action.

The bottom of the large pit was then covered with a fine layer of concrete, pink mortar and pebble, upon which the hypocaust was built. This required a main channel which enclosed a solid island of chalk blocks and clay. Although the surviving central block was not excavated it seems likely that it was about 0.80 × 2.00 m. in area. The channel enclosing this was probably 21–30 cm. wide and 50 cm. high. The sides were all lined with courses of chalk blocks and tiles set in brown clay, so that the combined island, main channels and linings formed a mass about 2 × 3 m. The voids left on each side of this central mass were then filled (S.8. L.8–14) with soil, mortar lumps and tile fragments, mostly in horizontal layers to avoid later slumping. A dump of pink-brown mortar (S.8. L.6 and S.9. L.6) capped these deposits.

The enclosing channel was linked to four other similar channels, each about 2.20 m. long, mostly 45 cm. high and 15–20 cm. wide, which radiated out to the four corners of the room. The largest was that leading to the south-east corner of the room where the stoke-hole is likely to have been positioned. These four channels, plus another smaller one joining the north-east channel, were all built of chalk blocks set in clay, but incorporating one or more courses of broken tiles, some laid diagonally (Fig. 8).

Each of the channel walls was topped by a large, mostly broken, flat tile. The tops of the channels were then sealed by large unbroken tiles, mostly 43 × 30 × 3 cm., in fact a standard Roman brick. At least 20 of these survived intact and several show clear animal paw-prints on them, occurring prior to firing. Once these capping tiles had been laid and the voids (S.8. L.7) filled in, the whole room was provided with a thick concrete floor (S.8. L.5), at least 10 cm. thick. This was constructed of white mortar and pebbles, with occasional tile chips and its surface was barely 30 cm. below the 1988 ground-level.

As regards dating evidence, about 60 sherds of coarse pottery were found sealed by the structure of the hypocaust itself, mostly in the packing behind the channel walls. The pottery (Nos. 111–113) includes three straight-sided dishes, two bead rim dishes, two flanged bowls and a variety of other forms. The dishes seem to be of a type dated A.D. 180–220 and the two bowls probably date from A.D. 200–250. Five sherds of samian ware, of Hadrianic-mid 3rd century date, were also found in the packing and confirm the dating of the coarse pottery. It seems clear from this that the hypocaust could not have been constructed before A.D. 200 and probably about A.D. 250, or even a little later.

The pottery from the filling of the hypocaust channels, some 24 sherds, includes a colour-coated beaker, two burnished cooking pots with outcurved rims and sherds of various fabrics (No. 114). Although some 1st and 2nd century vessels are included the latest pottery seems to date from the early-3rd century. Considering that the tiles over the hypocaust channels still remain intact, it seems likely that they were partly filled with soils containing earlier pottery. This event probably took place in the 4th century.

The Late Terrace (Fig. 7. S.13 and Fig. 5. S.1)
Another well-defined cut was detected along the west side of the Roman house, this time cutting through the fill of the very large Early Terrace. It was at least 15.30 m. in north-south length and mostly 1.20 m. wide from the west outside wall. It broadened out at the north end to a maximum width of 2.80 m. It must relate to the Period V building programme for its end coincides with the south end of the Period V new west wall (Room 16) and it also over-rides the wall of Room 15, not demolished until Period IV.

It had been filled progressively with a series of soils, mostly grey-brown loams (S.13. L.2–7), all containing some mortar and tile fragments. At the north end the terrace was substantially filled (S.1, L.12) with large fragments of roof tile, fallen from the roof over Room 9. This was then only being used as a stoke-hole for the Period V hypocaust and it seems that the roof here was serving little purpose and the tiles slid off in large numbers and were never recovered. Some 17 plain red tesserae were also found in the soils in this terrace.

As regards dating evidence nearly 300 potsherds were recovered from 11 deposits in the filling of this terrace. The great majority seems to be of Antonine date or into the early-3rd century (Nos. 115–116). Only two or three vessels seem to be of late-3rd century date and this contrasts with the earlier pottery. It seems likely that much of the soil being deposited here was derived, perhaps even coming from the slope above. The construction of the terrace itself, assigned to Period V, would anyway have removed earlier deposits and the upcast from this could have been placed on the uphill side.

The finds from these layers also included a bronze pin (No. 8), a bone pin (No. 16), a small marked chalk block (No. 30) and a small amount of animal bone.

The West Ditch (F1) (Plate XXV and Fig. 10)
The largest feature outside the Roman house was a substantial ditch, running roughly north–south on a straight alignment across the site. It lay uphill of the house and some 6.00–7.00 m. from it and being largely parallel to the walls. It seems to have served as a catchment drain for any storm-water coming down the hill above the house.

In detail, it was traced for over a distance of 25 m., which included a section 10 m. long under the existing driveway. Each end continued beyond the limits of the excavation and its total length is likely to have been greater than 50 m. It was generally 2.20–2.50 m. in width, some 30–70 cm. in depth and had steep or vertical sides and a broad, flat base. It was marginally wider and deeper at its north end and any quantity of water reaching it would have flowed north.

This feature clearly cut through earlier Roman soil deposits (Section A, L.5) and also through at least two features (Gully F54 and a clay-lined pit F67). It had silted substantially (Section A, L.1–3) before being re-cut towards its eastern end (Section B, L.1–2). This had also silted progressively with grey-brown sandy and clay loams, which contained domestic rubbish and charcoal specks. The overall ditch fill included 402 potsherds, five coins, fragments of tile and tesserae, five fragments of glass and 19 struck flint flakes.

The pottery is almost exclusively late-3rd and 4th century and the coins are all 4th century. The coins (Coin Nos. 13, 15, 21, 23–24) include one of Valens (A.D. 364–378), one of Valentinian I (A.D. 364–375) and three largely illegible, but almost certainly of 4th century date. They occur at both high and low levels and it seems that the ditch must have been dug, recut and fully silted during the 4th century A.D.

The pottery includes only eight sherds of samian ware, all survivals from the second half of the 2nd century. The coarse pottery also includes several vessels of 2nd century date, but the great majority is 4th century. Some 40 vessels (Nos. 123–129) include grog-tempered, sandy and colour-coated Oxfordshire wares whilst dishes, cooking pots and bowls are represented. The most common seem to be cooking pots with sharply everted rims and dishes or bowls with flanges or thickened rims. Four mortaria (Nos. 56–59) are included, all dated A.D. 240–400. Several small-finds, include the rim of a glass flagon (No. 34), part of a bronze bracelet (No. 6) and a possible toothpick/ear cleaner (No. 9).

Shaft F51 (Plate XXVI and Fig. 9)

This very deep pit, or shaft, was found largely outside the west wall of the Roman house, close to Room 8. It had been cut through the external Period I and Period II walls, through the internal Period III wall and floor and also through part of the layer of collapsed roof tile. Clearly, it related to a late phase of the Roman house.

It was oval in plan, 2.00 × 1.80 m. at the top and only 1.10 × 0.62 m. at the base. It had nearly vertical sides, a flat base and was about 2.95 m. in total depth. One half of the shaft had been excavated piecemeal over several seasons in the 1950's, but the other survived and was recorded. This showed a succession of some 22 largely horizontal layers of soil, mostly sands and clays, some containing flints and occasional tile.

Only 18 potsherds were recovered from the filling, mostly from the upper half. These are mostly well-fired sandy wares, but include a fragment of a comb-decorated cooking-pot of Farnham ware, a burnished dish (No. 117) with a token flange and two mortaria (No. 68). These seem to be common 4th century types. Other finds include a bronze finger-ring (No. 1) and a small fragment of a glass jar (No. 35). A single coin (Coin No. 19) was found in the upper fill of this shaft in 1960. This was a coin of Arcadius (A.D. 395), which helps confirm that the shaft could not have been completely filled before about A.D. 400. There was no thick silt at its base, just mostly sandy soils fallen in from the sides. It seems probable that this feature was filled not long after it was dug. Its unusual depth suggests that it may have been an attempt to excavate a well, but the total absence of any lining or progressive water-laid silt, suggests that it never served that purpose. Perhaps the water-table could not be reached and the sandy sides were too soft to permit a greater depth.

It is clearly significant that this large feature was dug partly across three walls and part of a floor. Clearly, this would have made its excavation very difficult and it seems clear that these particular walls were no longer standing when this was done. Had they been standing then the shaft could have been moved half a metre to avoid them.

Shaft F58 (Fig. 9)

This large feature, another deep pit or shaft, was found just outside the west wall of the Roman house close to Room 7. It was cut through part of the collapsed flint wall and also through the layer of fallen roof tile (L.15). Again, this was a feature relating to a late-Roman use of the site.

THE EXCAVATED STRUCTURES AND FEATURES 35

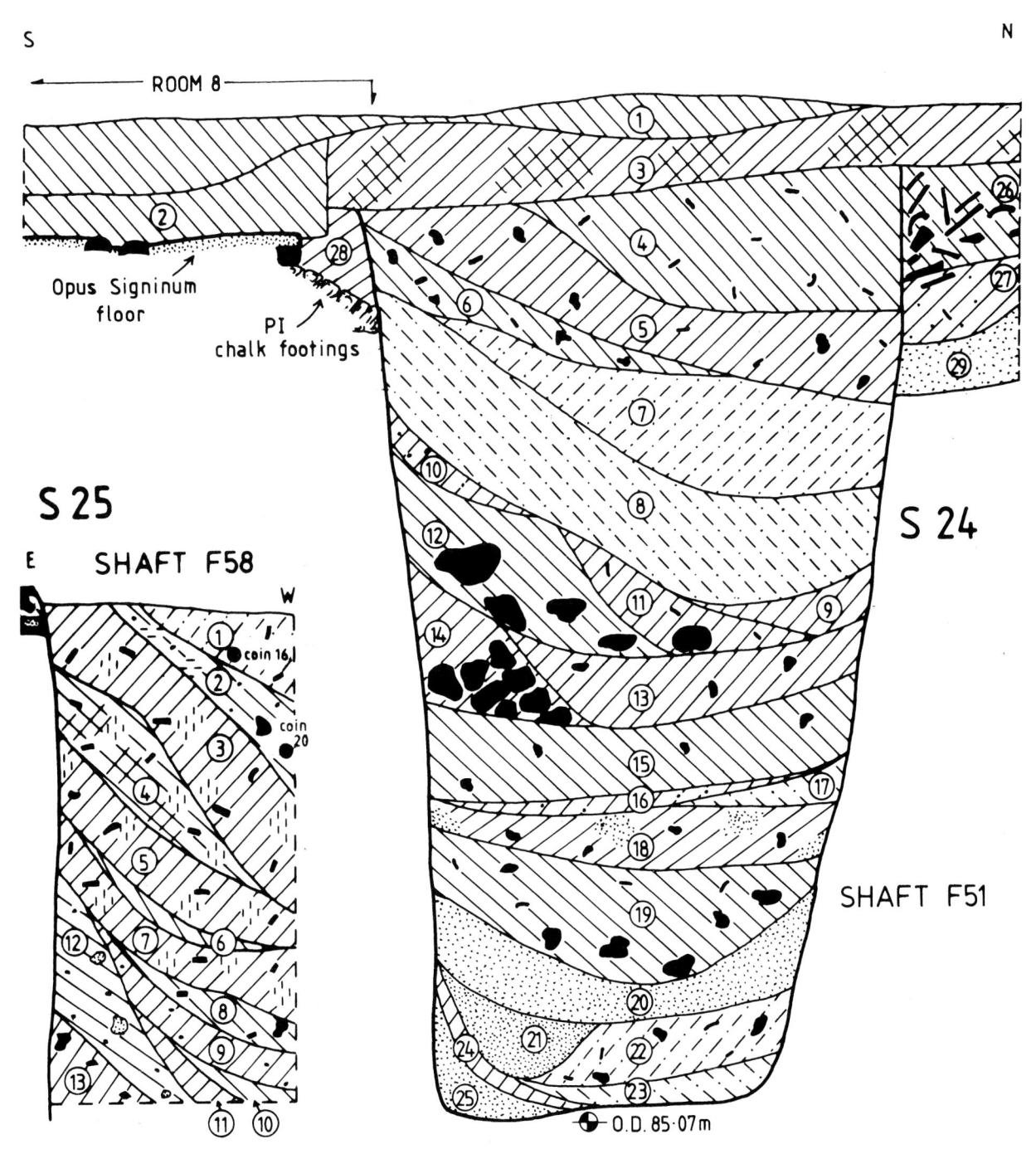

Fig. 9. Sections across shafts F51 and F58 (1/20)

It was oval in plan, measuring about 2.00 × 1.60 m. at the top, with near vertical sides. Due to the overhanging flint masonry it was only excavated to a depth of 1.73 m., which was clearly not the bottom. The bottom appears to have been reached in the 1950's when it was found to be over 2.00 m. deep. The western half was excavated then and only the north-east segment was excavated in 1988. This limited examination revealed a succession of sloping layers; sands, clays and some rubble (L.1–13). These seem to represent the deliberate filling of the upper part of this shaft.

A total of 182 fragments of pottery and two coins were found in the deposits examined. The coins (Coin Nos. 16 and 20) were of Valentinian I (A.D. 364–375) and Arcadius (A.D. 395–408). The pottery (Nos. 69–70 and 118–122) includes some of late-1st century date, several vessels of 2nd century date, but at least another ten vessels are 4th century. These include two colour-coated bowls and a sherd of a comb-decorated dolium of Farnham ware. Three more coins (Coin Nos. 1, 14 and 18) found in the shaft in 1961 were of Hadrian (A.D. 130), Valentinian (A.D. 364–375) and Theodosius (A.D. 379–395). From this it seems that the upper section of this shaft was filled at the end of the 4th century. It also seems that much earlier pottery was thrown into the shaft during the filling process, probably derived from rubbish-filled soil deposits nearby.

This deep pit, or shaft, may well have been another attempt to excavate a well on the site. This must have taken place sometime after the west wall had collapsed and after the tiles had slipped from the adjacent roof. Again it seems likely that this shaft was dug later in the 4th century and that it also failed to provide water.

The combined dating evidence from the site strongly suggests that Period V dated from about A.D. 270–300. It seems to have continued, without further detectable structural changes, until the end of the 4th century. It clearly post-dated the Period IV (A.D. 225–250) Room 14C, through which its own hypocausted Room 14D so substantially cut. The Late Terrace, dug to provide access to the back of the Period V house, contained late-3rd century pottery. In addition, the northern half of the villa, clearly abandoned during Period V, was partly buried under dumps containing pottery dating to A.D. 270–300. This could only have come from the Period V occupants. Of lesser significance, the Period IV Middle Terrace was filled and sealed by a soil layer containing three late-3rd century coins, perhaps dropped by the Period V occupants, or even the builders.

OTHER FEATURES AND DEPOSITS

Pits, Post-Holes and Ditches

At least 83 pits or post-holes were found at different points across the site, in addition to three large shafts or pits (see above). Of these 30 fall into four clear alignments (Pit-Lines A, B, C and D – see below), but the remainder were widely scattered, largely unrelated and of varying dates. These are tabulated below for simple reference, either as pits or post-holes. Two more relate to the medieval site and are described separately and three small ditches, or gullies, are also listed.

Pit-Line A (Fig. 11)

The largest features in the various pit-lines occur in a largely straight line on the north side of the large West Ditch (F1). Here some eight features were located, partly superimposed on each other and perhaps extending in both directions beyond the limits of the excavation. These again largely follow the line of the natural contour and are described below. None contained any real sign of ever having contained a post.

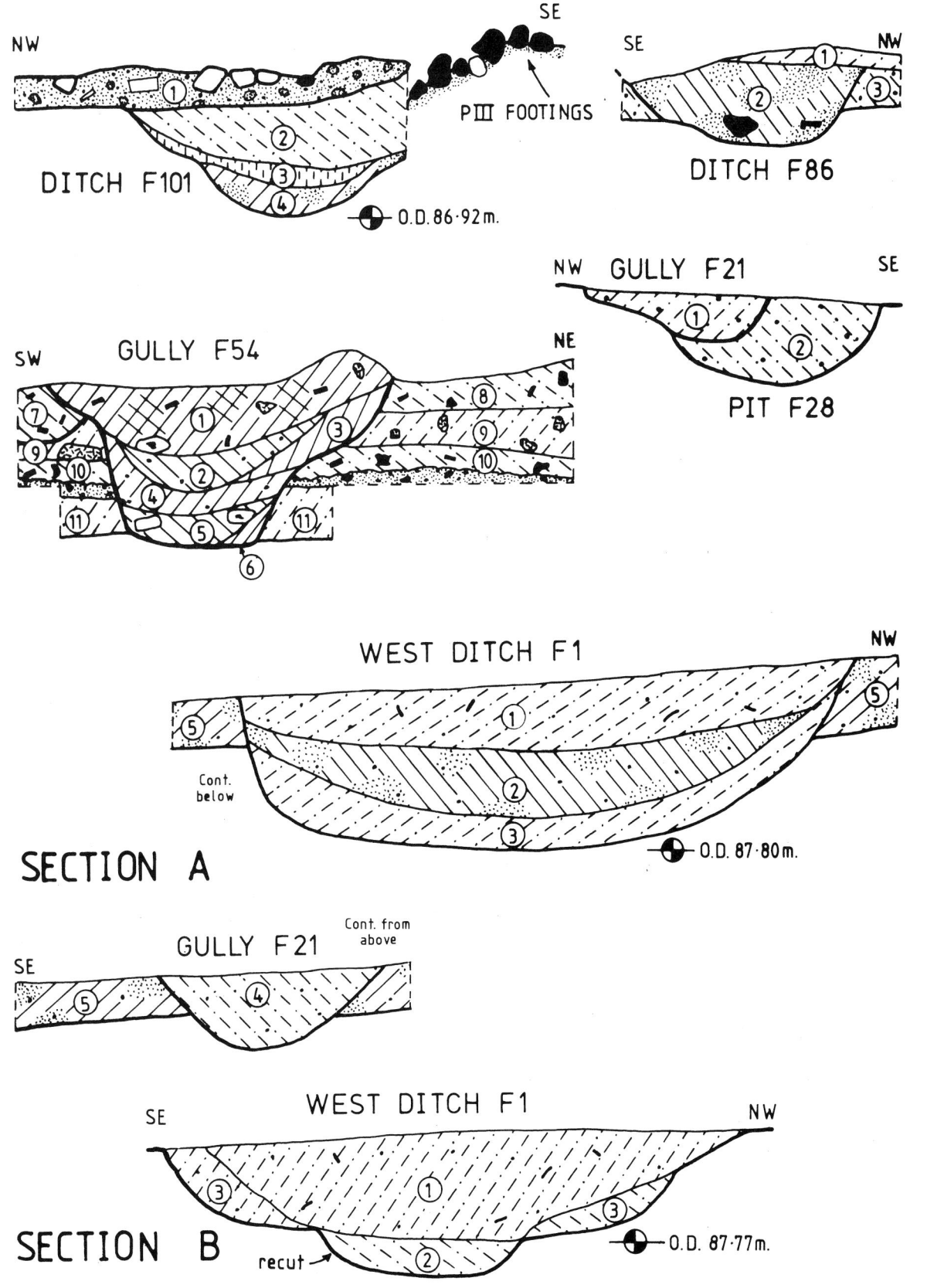

Fig. 10. Sections across Ditches and Gullies (1/20)

F. No.	Shape	Size	Depth	Sides	Base	Dep No.	Filling	Coarse Pot	Samian	Glass	Flint Flakes	Heat cracked Flint	Total
68	Oval	1.30 × 0.67	0.35 (min)	Steep	Flat	–	Mottled orange clay with brown loam	–	–	–	–	–	–
15	Oval	1.20 × 0.98	0.64 (min)	Sloping	Flat	203 38 204	Clay and loams with carbon and loam over orange clay with pebbles	4	–	3	–	–	7
3	Oval	1.10 × 1.00	0.95	Steep	Irreg.	17 41	Clay-loams with flint, pebbles and large flints	22	–	–	–	–	22
29	Sub-Rect	1.25 × 0.95	1.07	Steep	Flat	21 22 31 34 37	Clay-loams with flint and pebbles over sandy loam with pebbles	29	–	–	–	11	40
39	Oval	1.15 × 0.90 (min)	0.62	Vert/Steep	Flat	35 205	Clay-loams with pebbles	7	–	–	1	–	8
9	Oval	1.67 × 1.02	1.30	Vert	Flat	30 36 39 193	Clay-loams over sandy loams and pure sand.	32	2	2	5	–	41
14	Oval	1.32 × 1.12	1.12	Vert	Flat	42 38 203 204	Sandy loam and clays over pure sand with flint lumps and pebbles	11	–	–	–	–	11
10	Oval	1.28 × 0.80	0.39	Sloping	Rounded	33		4	–	–	–	–	4
							TOTALS	109	2	5	6	11	133

Table of Features in Pit-Line A

A study of these large pits seems to show five main groups. The earliest seems to be Pit F68 which was oval, shallow and contained no finds. When filled it was cut through by Pit F15, one of a series of four in line across the slope. The other pits were F3, 29 and 39. These were generally oval in plan, about 1.15 × 1.00 m., 0.62–1.07 m. deep, with steep sides and flat bases. The fillings were generally sandy loams, very similar to the natural sand through which they had been cut. There was no obvious trace of gradual silting or dumps of domestic rubbish and they appeared to have been filled not long after their excavation. Some 62 potsherds (Nos. 139–141) had gone back with this soil into the pits, mostly grog-tempered sherds of Patch Grove type, but including part of a poppy-head beaker, sherds of sandy ware cooking pots and a corky ware bead rim. All this pottery appears to be of late-first or early-second century date. Clearly, this filling could not have taken place much earlier than the middle of the second century A.D.

These four pits were spread across the site, centre to centre, Pit F15 being 3.00 m. from Pit F39. The latter was 2.00 m. from Pit F29, whilst this was 2.00 m. from Pit F3. A shallow hollow in the base of Pit F3 could suggest an earlier feature!

THE EXCAVATED STRUCTURES AND FEATURES 39

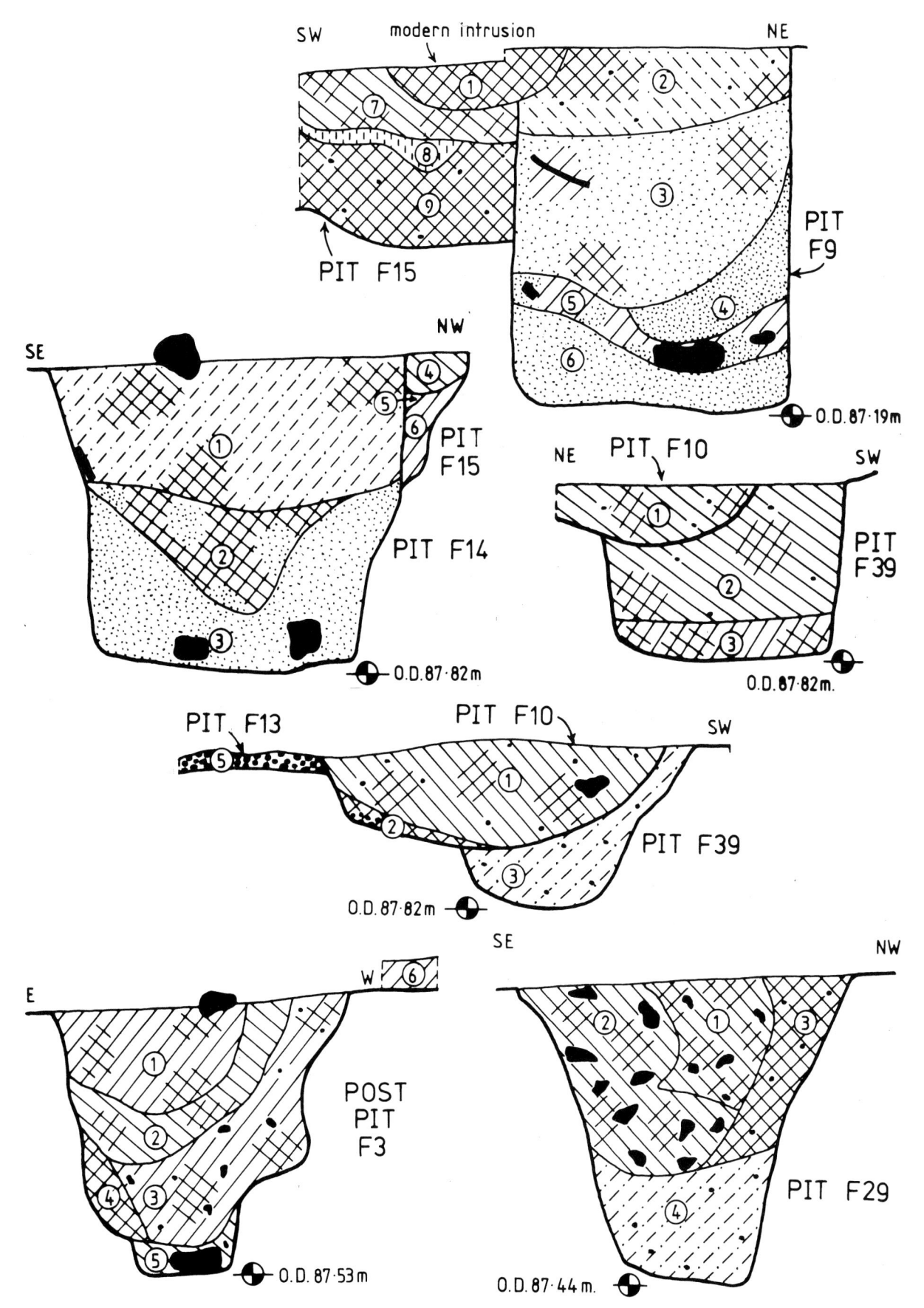

Fig. 11. Sections across Pit-Line A (1/20)

Pit 15 was clearly replaced by a pair of similar new pits (F9 and F14) which were rather larger and deeper. These too contained sandy soils, but also several large flints. Some 45 potsherds were recovered scattered throughout these pits and these included two samian vessels (Nos. 41 and 54) and a fragment of a large amphora. Most of the coarse pottery (Nos. 142–145) consists of native soft wares, similar to Patch Grove, but also includes a corky bead rim cooking pot, a sandy ware platter, a burnished dish and part of a large cream ware flagon. Again most seem to date prior to the middle of the second century, though one dish and a samian Form 31 (stamped) could be of Antonine date. The pits were about 1.50 m. apart, centre to centre.

Another pit (F10), similar in size but much shallower and with a different profile, was later cut through Pit F39. This contained four sherds of pottery including a mid-second century rim. It seems this pit did not otherwise relate to the others.

The precise function of these pits is difficult to gauge. At first glance the broadly similar size, alignment and fillings suggest that these were pits dug to contain massive wooden upright posts. Such posts occur frequently on Roman sites, as at Keston (Ref. 1) and Fordcroft (Ref. 2) nearby. However, in spite of careful excavation no clear evidence of post sockets was found and the general absence of packing stones is significant. The pits were not used for rubbish disposal and if they were used for underground storage, then some primary deposits should have been located. Their function must remain open.

Pit-Line B (Post-Holes) (Fig. 12 and Plate XXVII)
Another very well defined line of features was found between the Roman house and the large West Ditch. This consisted of eight roughly circular pits, seven of which contained central post-holes often packed with flints. This also ran roughly north–south and partly encroached across the fill of Gully F21. Most cut through the primary soil on the site.

On examination the post-pits were found to be mostly about 1.00 m. in diameter, 0.70–1.00 m. deep and had almost vertical sides and cupped bases. The post outlines, or pipes, were generally 27–64 cm. wide, suggesting that they held substantially circular posts averaging 30–50 cm. in diameter. The posts, centre to centre, were at intervals of 1.85–2.10 m.

The post-pits produced 48 potsherds (Nos. 146–151), again mostly native and sandy wares, but including parts of three beakers. The pottery dates from the late-first and second centuries, with the latest vessel, perhaps being a straight-sided dish with a burnished wavy line, dated to the late-second century. The post-pipes produced another 153 sherds, including a samian Form 31 of Antonine date. The coarse pottery is similar to that from the actual pits and indeed three vessels are identical. Again late-first and early-second century vessels predominate, but the presence of Antonine material and none of later date suggests that the posts were probably removed no later than about A.D. 180.

Pit-Line C (Fig. 13).
Yet another line of features, again running roughly north–south, was located and examined, this time only about 4 m. west of the outside wall of the Roman house. Here a line of six circular pits, all clearly containing medium sized post-holes, generally packed with flints, could be identified as belonging to a distinct series. Again others could have existed beyond the limits of the excavation. Five (F35, F40, F43, F45 and F93) lay west of the 1926 driveway and one (F55) lay at the edge of the railway embankment. The spacing, centre to centre, appears to have been about 2.50–2.90 m., but the southernmost two were about 4.00 m. apart.

F. No.	Shape	Size	Depth	Sides	Base	Dep No.	Filling	Coarse Pot	Samian	Flint Flakes
19 Post-Pit	Circ?	0.95 × 0.51 (min)	0.70	Steep	Cupped	48	Grey loam with flint and tile lumps	7	–	–
20 Post-Hole	Circ?	0.27 × 0.17 (min)	0.65 (min)	Vert	Cupped	49	Dark grey sandy loam with pebbles	4	–	–
17 Post-Pit	Oval	1.05 × 1.00	0.75	Vert	Cupped	47	Grey sandy loam with flints and pebbles over orange-grey loam	9	–	1
18 Post-Hole	Circ.	0.45 dia.	0.75	Vert	Rounded	46 188	Dark grey-brown sandy loam with flint lumps over grey sandy loam	25	–	–
63 Post-pit	Oval	1.05 × 0.90	0.72	Vert	Cupped	195 196	Orange-brown sandy loam over yellow-brown sandy loam	1	–	1
64 Post-Hole	Circ.	0.35 dia.	0.68	Vert	Cupped	–	Soft dark brown sandy loam	–	–	–
32 Post-Pit	Oval	1.10 × 0.89	0.88	Vert	Flat	–	Mottled yellow and brown sandy loam	–	–	–
33 Post-hole	Oval	0.70 × 0.58	0.88	Vert	Flat	54	Greeny-brown sandy loam with pebbles	64	–	1
30 Post-Pit	Oval	1.02 × 0.89	0.85	Vert	Rounded	104	Mixed yellow sand and brown loam	7	–	1
31 Post-Hole	Oval	0.64 × 0.62	0.68	Vert	Flat	53	Dark grey sandy loam, large flint and tile	37	–	–
47 Post-Pit	Oval	0.83 × 0.42	1.00 (min)	Vert	Rounded	99	Orange-brown sandy loam with flint and tile over orange-brown sandy loam	12	–	–
48 Post-Hole	Oval	0.50 × 0.37 (min)	0.73	Vert	Cupped	78	Mixed brown sandy loam and yellow sand and flint and tile	6	1 (F 31)	–
22 Post-Pit	Oval	1.20 × 1.00	0.84	Vert	Cupped	208 76	Brown sandy loam with flint and tile over light brown sandy loam with some flint	12	–	–
23 Post-Hole	Circ.	0.45 dia.	0.75	Vert	Cupped	77	Dark brown loam some flint and tile	13	–	–
24 Post-Pit	Oval	1.00 × 0.60 (min)	0.80	Steep	Rounded	80 81	Orange-brown sandy loam with flint and tile over a primary sandy brown loam	3	–	–
N.B. No Post-Hole associated with F24							TOTALS	200	1	4

Table of Features in Pit-Line B

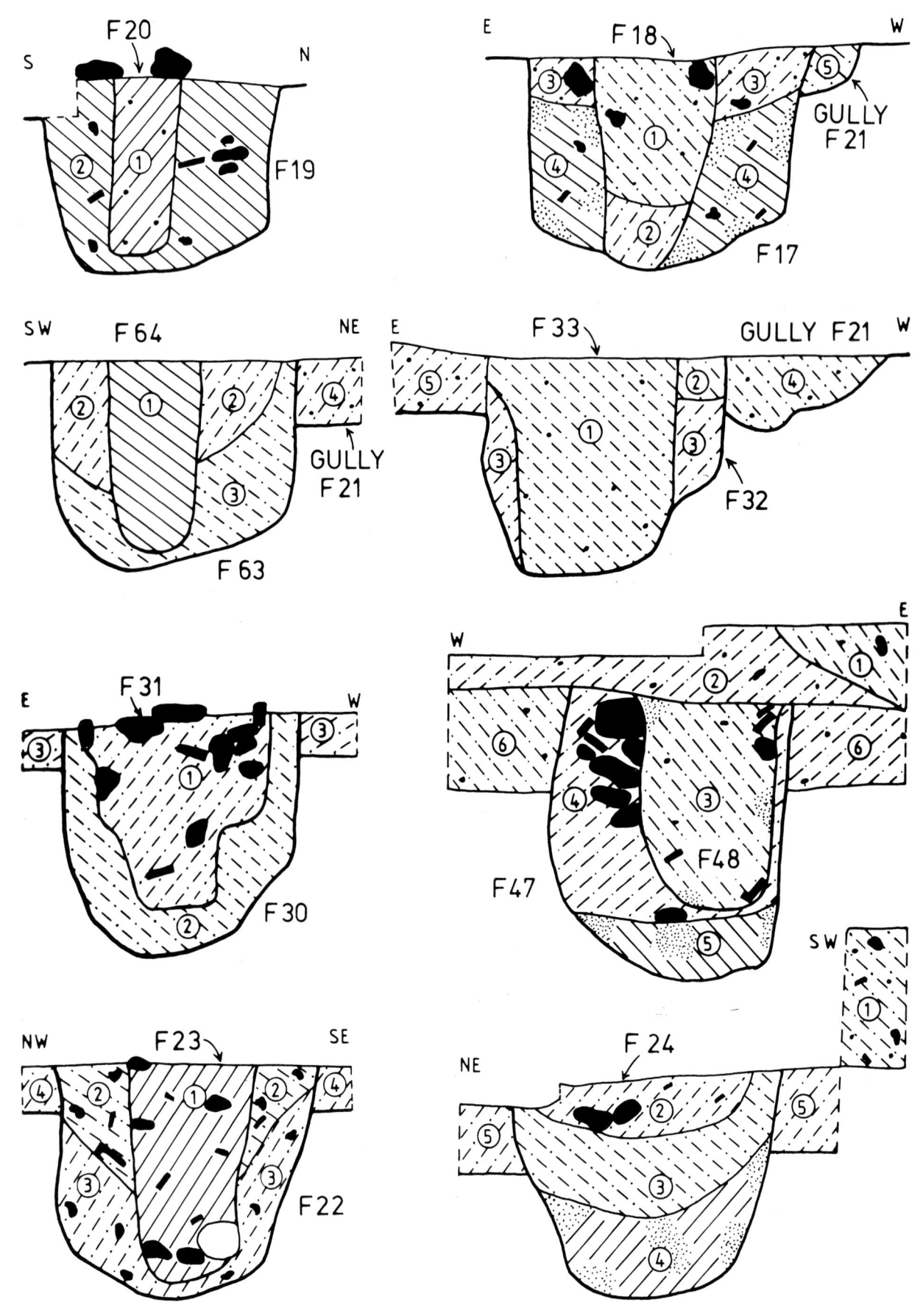

Fig. 12. Sections across Pit-Line B (1/20)

In detail the post-pits were mostly 46–68 cm. wide, 38–58 cm. deep and had steep or vertical sides. The posts were mostly 18–25 cm. wide and closely packed round with flint and tile.

As regards dating evidence it is clear that the post-pits had been dug through earlier soil deposits and were thus not associated with the earliest phase of activity. Some 34 potsherds were recovered from the pits and post-pipes. This included one sherd of samian ware (from Pit F40), a Form 31R of mid-late Antonine date. The coarse pottery is predominantly Roman sandy wares (Nos. 152–3) and of 2nd century date, whilst four vessels date from the end of that century. These include two plain burnished cooking pots and a colour-coated beaker with a cornice rim. Significantly, later pottery is absent and from this it seems likely that the posts had been removed about A.D. 200.

The posts seem to represent a substantial fence along the west side of the Roman house, probably replacing the much larger and earlier posts of Post-Line B.

F. No.	Shape	Size	Depth	Sides	Base	Dep. No.	Filling	Coarse Pot	Samian	Flint Flakes	Total
55 Post-Pit	Oval	0.88 × 0.80	0.48	Steep	Flat	–	Brown sandy clay and orange clay with flint lumps	–	–	–	–
56 Post-Hole	Oval	0.32 × 0.28	0.48	Vert	Flat	–	Brown sandy-loam, flint and tile over dark grey sandy loam	–	–	–	–
35 Post-Pit	Circ.	0.46 dia.	0.43	Vert	Cupped	111	Brown sandy-loam with many flints over green sand	1	–	–	1
36 Post-Hole	Circ.	0.20 dia.	0.38	Vert	Sloping	–	Dark brown sandy-loam small tile lumps and pebbles	–	–	–	–
40 Post-Pit	Oval	0.62 × 0.43	0.46	Steep	Pointed	52	Mottled orange-grey sandy-loam, many flint lumps	9	1 (F 31)	–	10
41 Post-Hole	Circ.	0.18 dia.	0.46	Vert	Pointed	51	Dark grey sandy-loam some flint and tile	15	–	1	16
43 Post-Pit	Circ.	0.50 dia.	0.45	Vert	Cupped	118	Light brown sandy-loam many large flint lumps	3	–	–	3
44 Post-Hole	Circ.	0.25 dia.	0.50	Vert	Cupped	–	Dark grey-brown sandy-loam some flint	–	–	–	–
45 Post-Pit	Oval	0.68 × 0.65	0.38	Steep/ Sloping	Rounded	206	Mottled yellow-brown sandy-loam over green sand	2	–	–	2
46 Post-Hole	Oval	0.25 × 0.20	0.35	Vert	Sloping	–	Brown sandy-loam	–	–	–	–
93 Post-Pit	Oval	0.55 × 0.27 (min)	0.50	Vert	Flat	282	Dark brown sandy-loam with flints and tile over orange-grey sandy-loam	3	–	–	3
							TOTALS	33	1	1	35

Table of Features in Pit-Line C

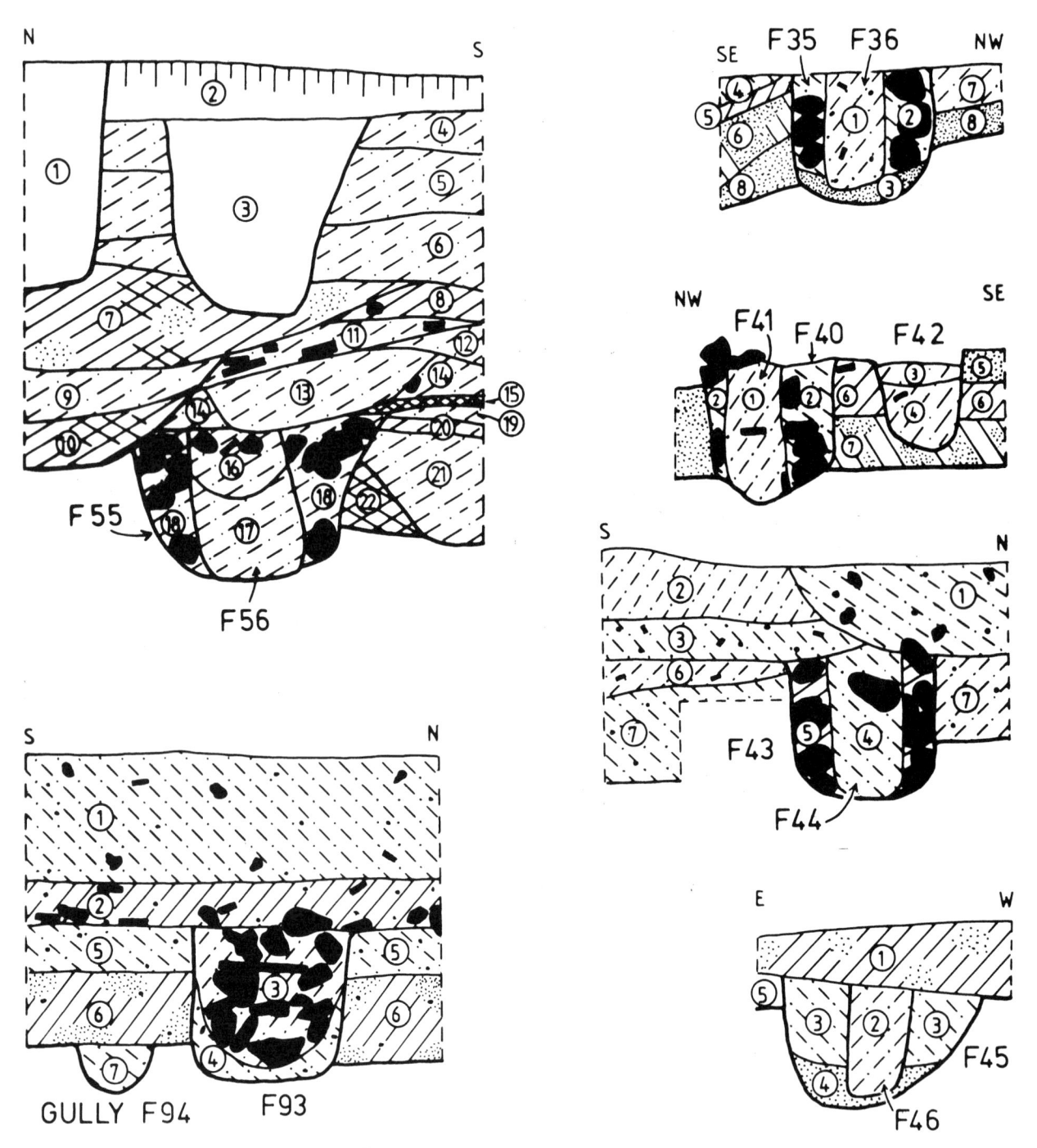

Fig. 13. Sections across Pit-Line C (1/20)

Pit-Line D (Fig. 14)

Another group of features, this time at the north end of the main area, just beyond Line A, seem largely to form another alignment. Of eight features here, six certainly fall on a north-south line with roughly equal spacing. Others could have existed beyond the limits of the excavation.

A close look at sizes, depths and contents suggests that three groups may be represented. Two pits (F5 and F6) are similar in size, are adjacent and contained no Roman material, but four and eight flints respectively. The flint includes six struck flakes, which are prehistoric in character. These features could be prehistoric and they do lie adjacent to an area of dense fire-cracked stone (F13 – see below).

F. No.	Shape	Size	Depth	Sides	Base	Dep. No.	Filling	Coarse Pot	Flint Flakes	Heat shattered Flints	Bone	Total
2	Oval	1.10 × 0.45	0.43	Sloping	Irreg.	15, 202	Sandy-loams with pebbles	4	–	–	–	4
12	Oval	0.45 × 0.34	0.07	Sloping	Rounded	–	Sandy-loam with pebbles	–	–	–	–	–
11	Oval	0.50 × 0.37	0.28	Steep	Flat	–	Sandy-loam	–	–	–	–	–
4	Oval	0.75 × 0.70	0.40	Steep	Irreg.	18	Clay-loams with much carbon	10	–	2	1	13
5	Oval	0.90 × 0.70	0.20	Sloping	Flat	19	Sandy-loam	–	3	1	–	4
6	Oval	1.05 × 0.65	0.13	Steep	Sloping	24	Sandy-loam with carbon specks	–	3	5	–	8
7	Circ.	0.22 dia.	0.17	Steep	Cupped	25	Loamy sand with carbon specks	–	2	1	–	3
25	Oval	0.56 × 0.54	0.30	Steep	Cupped	82	Sandy clay-loam	3	–	–	–	3
							TOTALS	17	8	9	1	35

Table of Features in Pit-Line D

Three more features (F2, 4 and 25) are similar and contained small amounts of Roman pottery. These were spaced across the site in a good line about 3.25 m. from each other, but no trace of posts was found in them. Only 17 potsherds were recovered, including a Patch Grove vessel, a poppyhead beaker and the bead rim of a small dish. This pottery seems to date from the middle of the second century.

Three more features (F7, 11 and 12) are much smaller and appear to be possible post-holes. One, F7, contained only two struck flint flakes and again could be prehistoric, being close to F13 containing the fire-cracked flints. The other two are close together, just 75 cm. apart and although devoid of finds they seem to relate to the line of the three Roman pits.

Fig. 14. Sections across Pit-Line D (1/20)

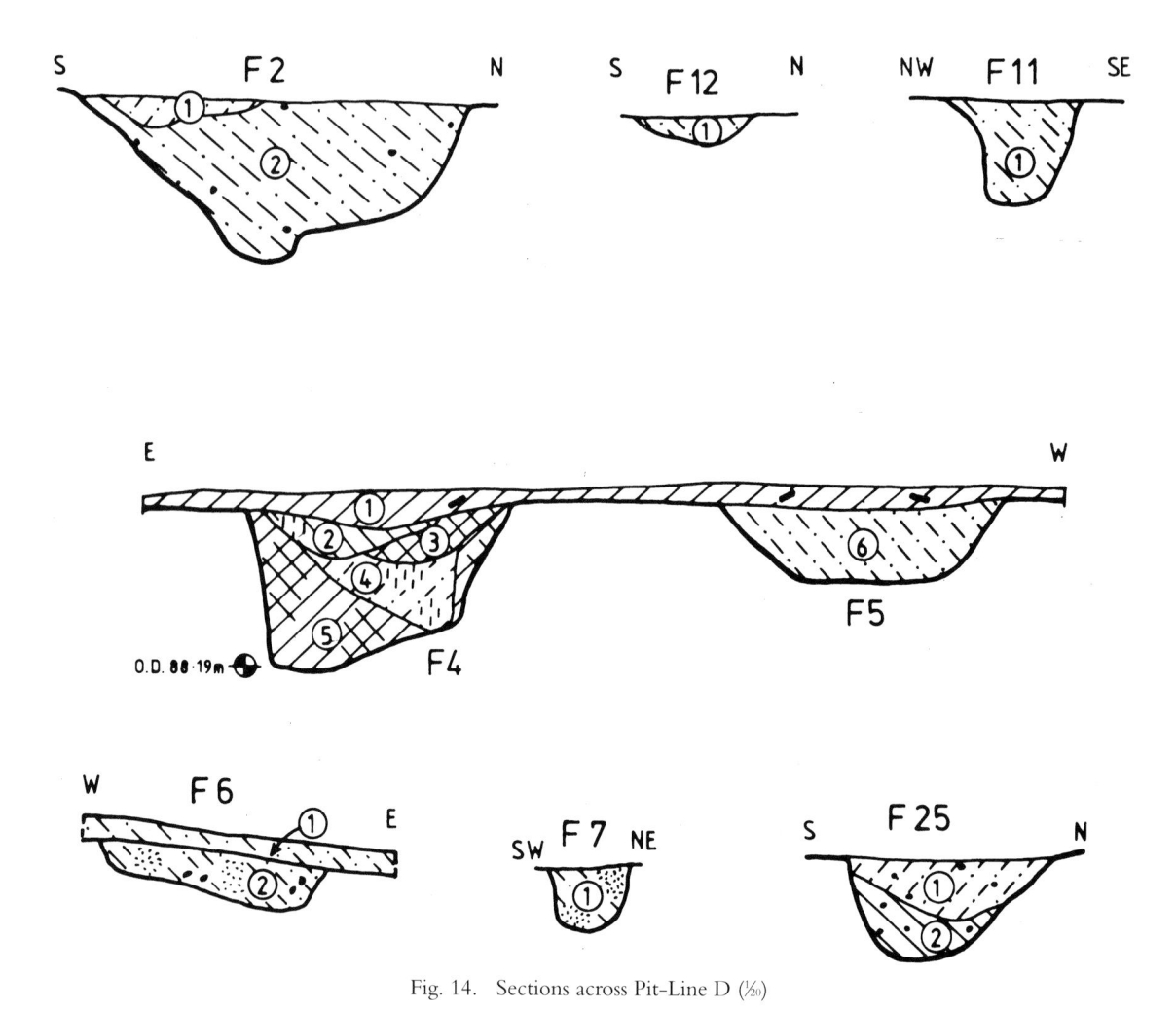

All this suggests that three of the features could be prehistoric in date, but three of the pits on a good alignment could just have formed a small Roman boundary-fence, whilst the pair of post-holes on the same alignment could represent extra support, or even a small gateway. This might then date to the middle of the second century.

Miscellaneous Pits ((Fig. 15)
Another 35 pits, of varying sizes, dates and functions, were located across the site and these are listed below. Most contained few or no dateable objects and only five had more than 10 potsherds.

THE EXCAVATED STRUCTURES AND FEATURES 47

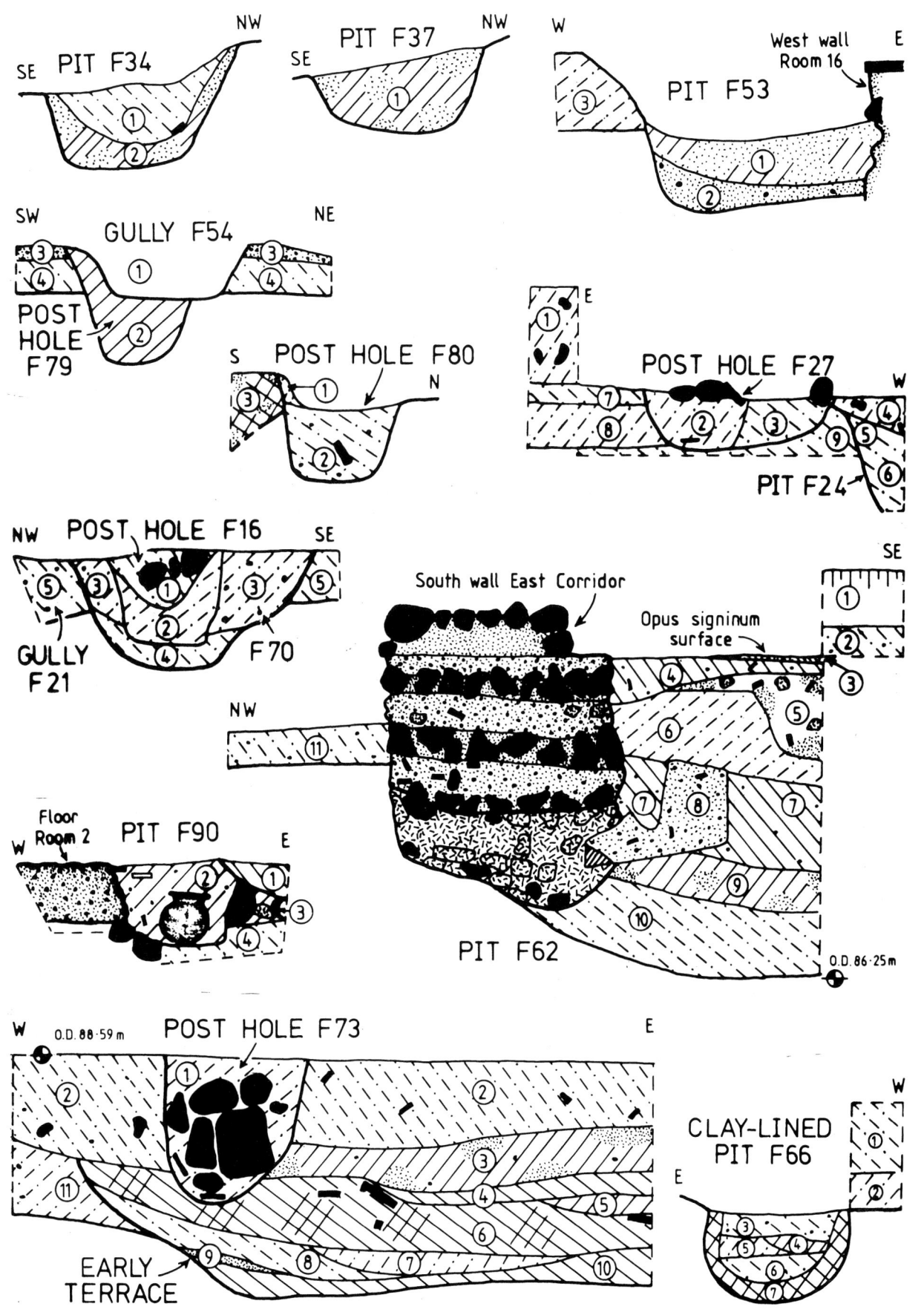

Fig. 15. Sections across miscellaneous Pits and Post-holes (1/20)

F. No.	Shape	Size	Depth	Sides	Base	Filling	Dep. No.	Coarse Pot	Samian	Mortaria	Flint	Other
8	Oval	0.52 × 0.45	0.16	Sloping	Rounded	Clay-lined pit lining = green clay:fill = dark grey sandy-loam	29	1 (No. 154)	–	–	–	–
13	Irreg.	1.65 × 1.10 (min)	0.07 (min)	Shallow	Flat	Heat shattered flints with carbon and black loam	197	–	–	–	–	33
28	Oval?	0.75 × 0.52 (min)	0.30	Sloping	Rounded	Grey-orange sandy-loam. Orange clay patches and pebbles	–	–	–	–	–	–
34	Oval	0.76 × 0.70	0.44	Sloping	Flat	Light brown sandy-loam	–	–	–	–	–	–
37	Circ.	0.64 dia.	0.30	Sloping	Flat	Yellow sand and light brown loam	–	–	–	–	–	–
53	Oval	0.82 × 0.74	0.24 (min)	Steep	Flat	Yellow sand and brown loam	125	3	–	–	–	–
60	Oval?	0.52 × 0.42 (min)	0.12	Sloping	Rounded	Grey-brown sandy-loam	–	–	–	–	–	–
61	Oval?	0.60 × 0.40 (min)	0.40	Sloping	Rounded	Brown loam, carbon and burnt clay	143	–	–	–	–	6 daub
65	Oval	1.45 × 0.78	0.40	Sloping	Pointed	Dark brown sandy-loam, flint lumps	198	1	–	–	–	–
66	Circ?	0.52 × 0.40 (min)	0.30	Sloping	Rounded	Clay-lined pit lining = orange-grey clay:filling = Brown sandy clays	199 200	–	–	–	5	–
67	Circ?	0.65 × 0.45 (min)	0.25	Steep	Cupped	Clay-lined pit lining = orange-grey clay. Filling = Light brown sandy clays	–	–	–	–	–	–
71	Circ.	0.57 dia.	0.17	Steep	Flat	Light brown sandy-loam	–	–	–	–	–	–
72	Circ.	0.60 dia.	0.17	Steep	Flat	Yellow-brown sandy-loam	–	–	–	–	–	–
74	Oval	0.49 × 0.47	0.36	Sloping	Irreg.	Grey-brown clay-loam	272	1	–	–	–	–
76	Oval	0.62 × 0.50	0.10	Sloping	Flat	Light brown clay-loam	237	3	–	–	1	–
78	Oval	0.90 × 0.63	0.23	Sloping	Irreg.	Light brown clay	248	15 (No. 158)	–	–	–	–
84	Circ?	0.50 × 0.30 (min)	0.30	Sloping	Rounded	Green-brown loam	254	3	–	–	–	–
85	Oval	0.50 × 0.47	0.14	Steep	Flat	Grey-brown clay and articulated animal bones	227	2	–	–	–	159 sheep skeleton
87	Sub-Rect.	1.20 × 0.95	0.20	Sloping	Flat	Grey clay-loams angular flint	259 265	107 (Nos. 160–1)	–	No. 63	2	16 glass
88	Circ.	0.52 dia.	0.30	Sloping	Rounded	Brown sandy-loam	260	6	–	–	2	–

F. No.	Shape	Size	Depth	Sides	Base	Filling	Dep. No.	Coarse Pot	Samian	Mortaria	Flint	Other
90	Oval	0.50 × 0.45	0.29	Sloping	Flat	Brown gritty loam	275	1 (No. 159)	–	–	–	–
91	Oval	0.32 × 0.23	0.08	Sloping	Rounded	Mixed orange-brown sandy-loam	283	1	–	–	–	–
92	Sub-Square	0.52 × 0.20	– (min)	–	–	–	–	–	–	–	–	–
95	Oval	1.10 × 0.86	0.35	Sloping	Rounded	Dark brown loam	156	66 (Nos. 155–6)	2 (F 31)	No. 61	–	1 glass
96	Oval	1.05 × 1.60 (min)	0.23 (min)	Sloping	Flat	Dark green-brown loam and flint lumps	261	1	–	–	–	–
97	Oval	0.63 × 0.29	0.75 (min)	Sloping	Flat	Mottled brown and yellow sandy-loam	–	–	–	–	–	–
98	Circ.?	2.06 dia.	0.43	Sloping	Cupped	Brown sandy clay-loam	286	8 (No. 157)	–	–	–	–
99	Sub-circ.	0.60 × 0.20 (min)	0.49	Steep	Sloping	Light brown sandy clay	287	1	–	–	–	–
100	Circ.	0.48 dia.	0.25	Sloping	Rounded	Grey-brown sandy-loam	106	3	–	–	–	19 Bone
103	Circ.?	0.82 dia.	0.25	Sloping	Cupped	Grey-brown mixed sandy-loams	150	–	–	–	2	–
105	Circ.	0.38 dia.	0.46	Steep	Cupped	Green-brown sandy-loam	127	30	–	–	–	–
107	Oval	1.38 × 0.94	1.20	Steep	Rounded	Brown-cream loam with bands of charcoal and yellow sand	335 342 343	45 (Nos. 162–4)	3 (F 36, 18/31)	–	–	7 iron 7 antler 5 tile (No. 25)
111	Oval?	0.39 × 0.30 (min)	0.05	Sloping	Flat	Mixed brown clay and yellow sand	–	–	–	–	–	–
112	Oval	0.65 × 0.50	0.45	Sloping	Flat	Compact opus signinum and painted plaster	345	–	–	–	–	1 plaster
115	Circ.	0.45 dia.	0.35	Vert.	Cupped	Black-brown loam	346	2	–	–	1	–
						TOTALS		280	5	2	12	40

Table of Miscellaneous Pits

Miscellaneous Post-Holes (Fig. 15).

A total of 18 more post-holes were found at different points across the site and again vary in date, size and detail. They contained few or no dateable objects and are listed below.

F. No.	Shape	Size	Depth	Sides	Base	Dep. No.	Filling	Coarse Pot	Samian	Flint Flakes	Tile	Glass	Total
70 Post-Pit	Oval	0.90 × 0.80	0.43	Steep	Rounded	–	Brown sandy-loam, occ. pebbles.	–	–	–	–	–	–
16 Post-Hole	Oval	0.42 × 0.38	0.34	Vert.	Flat	44 45	Dark grey sandy-loam and flint lumps.	7 (No. 170)	–	2	–	–	9
27 Post-Hole	Oval	0.54 × 0.17	0.20	Sloping	Flat	79	Cream-brown sandy-loam flint lumps.	1	1 (No. 50)	–	–	–	2
42 Post-Hole	Oval	0.32 × 0.29	0.33	Steep	Rounded	112 113	Dark brown sandy clay-loam with tile lumps.	8 (No. 172)	–	–	–	–	8
50 Post-Hole	Circ.	0.34 dia.	0.18	Sloping	Cupped	–	Dark brown sandy-loam. Some flint and chalk.	–	–	–	–	–	–
52 Post-Socket	Oval	0.27 × 0.25	0.14	Steep	Flat	–	Dark brown clay-loam, daub and tile.	–	–	–	–	–	–
57 Post-Hole	Circ?	0.25 dia.	0.22	Vert.	Flat	–	Dark brown sandy-loam and flint.	–	–	–	–	–	–
69 Post-Hole	Circ.	0.44 dia.	0.48	Steep	Cupped	92 110	Dark grey-brown sandy loam tile, mortar and chalk.	9 (No. 171)	–	–	–	–	9
73 Post-Hole	Circ?	0.53 dia.	0.52	Vert.	Pointed	91	Light grey sandy clay-loam with large flint, tile.	1	–	–	–	6	7
79 Post-Hole	Circ.	0.42 dia.	0.25	Steep	Rounded	249	Light grey, clay-loam, op. sig., mortar, chalk tile and flint.	1	–	–	1	–	2
80 Post-Hole	Circ.	0.52 dia.	0.25	Steep	Cupped	250	Mottled brown sandy clay-loam, flint pebbles and tiles.	–	–	–	1	–	1
89 Post-Hole	Oval	0.46 × 0.40	0.30	Steep	Flat	270	Orange clay with pebbles.	6	–	–	–	–	6
106 Post-Hole	Circ.	0.39 dia.	0.17	Steep	Rounded	333	Mixed brown and yellow sandy-loam, carbon specks.	2	–	–	–	–	2
108 Post-Hole	Oval	0.21 × 0.19	0.13	Steep	Cupped	344	Brown sandy loam, carbon specks, tile.	3	–	1	1	–	5
109 Post-Hole	Circ.	0.18 dia.	0.06	Sloping	Rounded	–	Brown sandy-loam, carbon specks.	–	–	–	–	–	–

F. No.	Shape	Size	Depth	Sides	Base	Dep. No.	Filling	Coarse Pot	Samian	Flint Flakes	Tile	Glass	Total
110	Post-Hole	Oval	0.20 × 0.18	0.06	Sloping	Rounded	–	Brown loam, carbon specks, chalk, mortar, tile.	–	–	–	–	–	–
113	Post-Hole	Circ.	0.10 dia.	0.15	Vert.	Flat	–	Dark brown loam carbon specks.	–	–	–	–	–	–
114	Post-Hole	Circ.	0.15 dia.	0.20	Vert.	Cupped	–	Dark brown loam, carbon specks.	–	–	–	–	–	–
							TOTALS	38	1	3	3	6	51

Table of Miscellaneous Post-Holes

Miscellaneous Ditches (Fig. 10)

Three more small ditches, or gullies, were also found during the excavation and these are listed below. Two (F54 and F81) were on the railway embankment and the other (F86) was a gully draining into a terrace behind the villa.

F. No.	Length	Width	Sides	Base	Dep. No.	Filling	Coarse Pot	Samian	Other
54	3.90 (min)	1.20	Sloping	Flat	168 251 255 256	Grey loam, over gritty loams	49 (Nos. 165–167)	1	Bone pin (No. 19) Flint
81	5.40 (min)	0.95	Sloping	Flat	246 267	Brown sandy-loam with tile and mortar	53 (Nos. 168–9)	1	Bronze (No. 12)
86	1.90 (min)	1.00	Sloping	Cupped	262	Brown sandy-loam with pebbles	1	1	–

Table of Miscellaneous Ditches/Gullies

GENERAL LAYERS SEALING THE VILLA

A series of widely scattered soil deposits sealed different parts of the Roman house and these contained substantial quantities of rubble and domestic rubbish. These were initially thought to represent the 'final demolition' of the house and contain exclusively late-Roman material.

An examination of the pottery and contexts, however, suggests varying circumstances, including deep post-Roman disturbance and soil dumping. Effectively, most of the contents of these deposits must be regarded as unstratified.

Some 18 layers contained about 900 potsherds and nearly 300 miscellaneous objects. The pottery includes 43 sherds of samian (Nos. 43–6, 49, 52), mostly Antonine-mid 3rd century; 9 fragments of mortaria (Nos. 66–7), over 800 fragments of coarse pottery (Nos. 130–138), a 3rd century coin (Coin No. 8) and over 100 tesserae. The small-finds include an ear-scoop (No. 11), a bone pin (No. 20) and part of part of a shale dish (No. 28).

Whilst some of the coarse pottery is of 2nd century date, the bulk appears to be of late- 3rd or 4th century date. It adds little to the structural history of the villa and generally confirms the date-range of the material from the stratified deposits.

THE UNSTRATIFIED DEPOSITS

Inevitably, on a site so disturbed by earlier building-work and excavations, many soil deposits cannot be regarded as sealed or stratified. These contained a substantial number of objects and include two coins (Coin Nos. 10 and 25), one of Constans (A.D. 337–350) and one of George V (1920) and some bronze tweezers (No. 15). The pottery includes about 480 coarse ware potsherds, very largely reflecting the rest of the pottery from the site both in type and date. A few sherds are clearly of 19th century date and six sherds are from a large jug, probably of 14th century date. This is green glazed and decorated with a series of small applied stars. Some 30 samian ware vessels (Nos. 47–48 and 51) are mostly Hadrian-Antonine, but include some of late-1st century date and some of early-3rd century date.

Much of the pottery from the 1950's excavation is difficult to relate to the 1988 stratification with certainty. Of the 12 coins found then, five can be related to features or rooms, but seven more (Coins Nos. 5, 6, 7, 9, 11, 12, 17) are substantially unstratified. These are two of Carausius (A.D. 287–293), one of Constans (A.D. 337–350), one of Constantius II (A.D. 355–360), one of Gratian (A.D. 367–383) and two of 3rd or 4th century date.

C. THE POST-ROMAN PERIOD

The latest Roman coins on the site are two of Arcadius (Coin Nos. 19–20), minted at the very end of the 4th century and lost then, or later. These suggest the site was still at least partially occupied then and it seems likely that it had ceased to function no later than the opening decades of the 5th century. Decay must have soon set in and very large numbers of roof-tiles slid off the west side of the house (Plate XXVIII).

It is also clear that the remains of the Roman house subsequently became buried under a steady wash of soil from the hillside above, probably over many centuries. A layer of largely sterile soil, mostly 40–60 cm. deep (S.1, L.11, 17) eventually covered the building and the fallen roof-tiles. This deep layer must have made the structure invisible at ground-level, with the walls already removed for building work elsewhere.

Of very special interest here was the discovery of a large pit containing hearths, cut down into the hillwash over the villa. This was the first feature revealed when the topsoil was removed and nearby were two small post-holes (see below).

The Hearth (F77) (Plate XXIX and S.1)

In detail the hearth had been built inside a sub-rectangular pit about 1.80 × 1.60 m. and mostly 50 cm. deep. The pit had vertical sides, a largely flat base and actually cut into the fill of the underlying Roman terraces. The hearth (L.9) was oval in plan and showed as an area of intense orange-black burning, about 1.30 × 0.95 m., on the west side of the pit. This was sealed by a layer of burnt clay fragments and charcoal (L.7), which in turn was sealed by a second hearth (L.6), burnt hard. This measured about 90 × 60 cm. This was covered and the rest of the pit filled by a substantial deposit of fragmented burnt daub, grey loam and charcoal specks (L.3–5). Clearly, the pit had been deliberately filled in a single operation. It seems likely that the pit was large enough for the person controlling the fire to stand in it. Clearly, this was a carefully constructed feature which, in the absence of industrial debris, was probably used for cooking or more likely for baking.

The various layers forming in, around and sealing the hearth within this large pit contained about 50 potsherds. The majority is clearly Roman (Nos. 174–5) and small in size, but the feature is stratigraphically very much post-Roman in date and these must have been derived from the lower deposits. Of special interest, however, are some 17 sherds of a single vessel (No. 173) of shell-loaded ware with an outcurved rim. This seems to be of 11th–12th century date and it must have been thrown into the pit with the large amount of daub. Considering the substantial size of some of the sherds from this vessel and the vertical stratigraphy, it seems clear that the pit and hearths were constructed about the 11th–12th centuries. A single fragment of Roman vessel glass (No. 31) was also found in the pit filling.

Some 21 of the largest fragments of daub were retained. These had not come from the oven, but must have come from an adjacent wattle-and-daub structure, that was burnt down and the debris thrown into the pit. The daub is made of sandy clay containing occasional pebbles. Most is orange-brown in colour, but some is buff-coloured. Most of the fragments have an uneven back and show very clear imprints of wattles at the broken fronts. The wattle imprints are nearly all circular and vary in diameter from 10–25 cm., the majority being 15–20 cm. Where there is more than one imprint they mostly run roughly parallel, but in some cases the imprints are at right-angles to each other. A rough trellis of thin branches is indicated, perhaps held within a larger frame of posts and cased in thick clay. The surviving fragments are 3–5 cm. thick and if these had broken along the centres, then the original thickness was probably 6–10 cm. It is likely that the fragments represent the vertical walls of a building which stood nearby in the 11th–12th centuries A.D. It is just possible that the pit with its hearths stood inside such a structure, for the vertical sides of the pit had not weathered down and seem to have been protected in some way. The total absence of similarly dated pottery and daub on this large site is significant and suggests that, perhaps, more was removed by later ploughing and other activity. Clearly, had this material not been discarded into this large pit no trace whatever would have survived.

Post-Hole F26
This oval-shaped hole partly cut into the daub fill of the 11th–12th century pit and must therefore be of later date. It was 52 × 48 cm. in area, 40 cm. deep and had sloping sides and a rounded base. Its filling of grey loam contained pebbles, tile fragments and a sherd of Roman pottery. Several large flints at its sides probably packed a central post of uncertain size.

Post-Hole F49
Another oval-shaped post-hole probably formed a pair with the one cutting the pit, for it too cut the deep hillwash deposits, was of similar size and lay about 3.25 m. to the north-west. It was about 70 × 60 cm., some 45 cm. deep and had sloping sides and a flat base. Its filling of sandy loam produced a single potsherd. This was from a green-glazed jug, probably of 14th century date. If these two high-level post-holes did relate together, as seems likely, then they could have formed part of a medieval structure of unknown size or extent, perhaps dating from the 14th century. Part of another green-glazed jug, also probably of 14th century date, was found unstratified at the edge of the railway cutting.

The 1955–7 excavations are reported to have found part of a Saxon glass cone-beaker, an iron knife dated by Norman Cook to 11th–12th centuries and a sherd of another medieval jug.

The hearth and pottery in it seem to date from 11th–12th centuries and strongly suggest the presence here of a domestic settlement, perhaps with the hearth being within a structure. The two later post-holes suggest another structure which the associated pottery suggests was no later than 14th century in date. Taken together these features and finds all point to a settlement here in the 10th–14th centuries, perhaps a farmstead or larger. This could in fact identify it with the lost site of 'Croctune', recorded in the Domesday Survey of 1086 and certainly in this general area (see discussion).

54 THE ROMAN VILLA SITE AT ORPINGTON, KENT

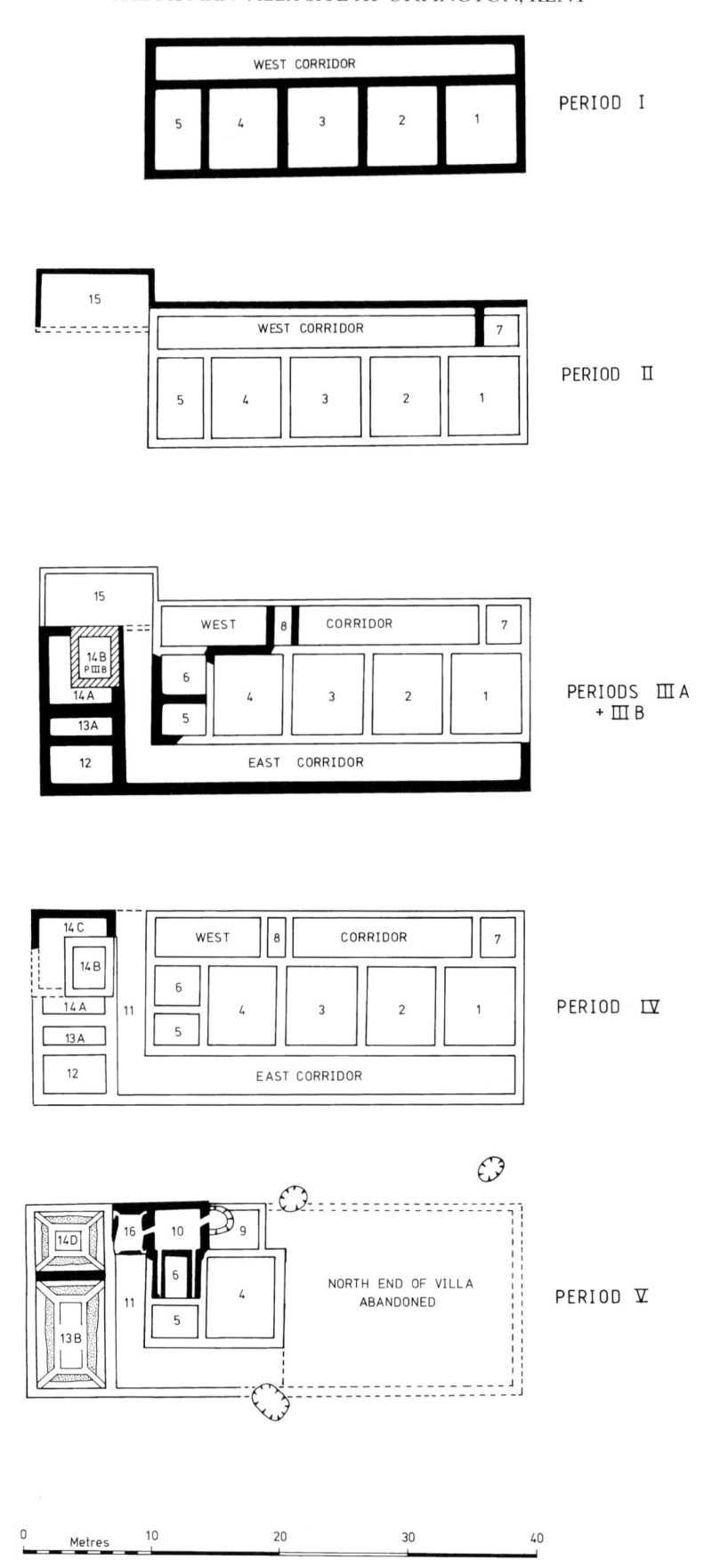

Fig. 16. Plans showing development of Villa, Periods I–V

CHAPTER III

THE EXCAVATED OBJECTS

A. THE COINS

Only 13 coins were recovered during the 1988–89 excavation and to these can be added another 12 from the 1950's work. A total of 24 Roman coins is thus produced which is a small number for a major villa site. However, the site had been substantially cleared in the 1927 excavation and damaged by the construction of the driveways, the railway cutting and later road, so others will certainly have been lost.

This small number is of little use for general comment and the coin-loss is unlikely to be a fair reflection of the occupation over at least three centuries. Indeed, this can be seen clearly when the coins are compared with the pottery. The latter is vastly greater in quantity and must more fairly represent the occupation of the site. Probably over 50% of the pottery found dates from the second half of the second century, whereas only one coin could have been lost during that time. Almost predictably 96% of the coins date from about A.D. 270–400, whereas perhaps roughly 30% of the pottery is of that date.

Perhaps the only real value that this small collection has, apart from the 16 which were stratified, is that it demonstrates coin-loss on the site right up until the end of the fourth century A.D. There seems little doubt from these coins that the villa was still active in some form at about A.D. 400, or even a little later.

Coin No.	Exc. No. 1955–61	Exc. No. 1988–9	Emperor	Date A.D.	Feature/Context	K.F. No.	Deposit No.
1	12	–	Hadrian	130	Shaft F58	–	–
2	–	11	Gallienus	260–268	Over PIV Terrace	28	310
3	9	–	Barbarous (Imit. Tetricus I)	270–273	On floor of Room 8	–	–
4	–	12	Barbarous (Rad)	270–290	Over PIV Terrace	29	310
5	3	–	Carausius	287–293	Unstratified	–	–
6	7	–	Radiate Imitation Carausius	287–293	Unstratified	–	–
7	2	–	Illegible	3rd C	Unstratified	–	–
8	–	3	Illegible	3rd C	Soils sealing Villa	3	61
9	4	–	Constans	337–350	Unstratified	–	–
10	–	5	Constans	337–350	Unstratified	10	2
11	8	–	Constantius II	355–360	Unstratified	–	–
12	5	–	Barbarous	355–365	Unstratified	–	–
13	–	1	Valens	364–378	Ditch F1	1	26
14	6	–	Valentinian I	364–375	Shaft F58	–	–
15	–	4	Valentinian I	364–375	Ditch F1	5	10
16	–	10	Valentinian I	364–375	Shaft F58	18	212
17	1	–	Gratian	367–383	Unstratified	–	–
18	11	–	Theodosius	379–395	Shaft F58	–	–
19	10	–	Arcadius?	395?	Shaft F51	–	–
20	–	6	Arcadius	395–408	Shaft F58	12	147
21	–	8	Uncertain	3–4th C	Ditch F1	16	12
22	–	13	Uncertain	3–4th C	Over PIV Terrace	30	310
23	–	9	Uncertain	4th C	Ditch F1	22	12
24	–	2	Uncertain	Late-4th C	Ditch F1	2	27
25	–	7	George V	1920	Disturbed	13	86

Table of Coins from the Site

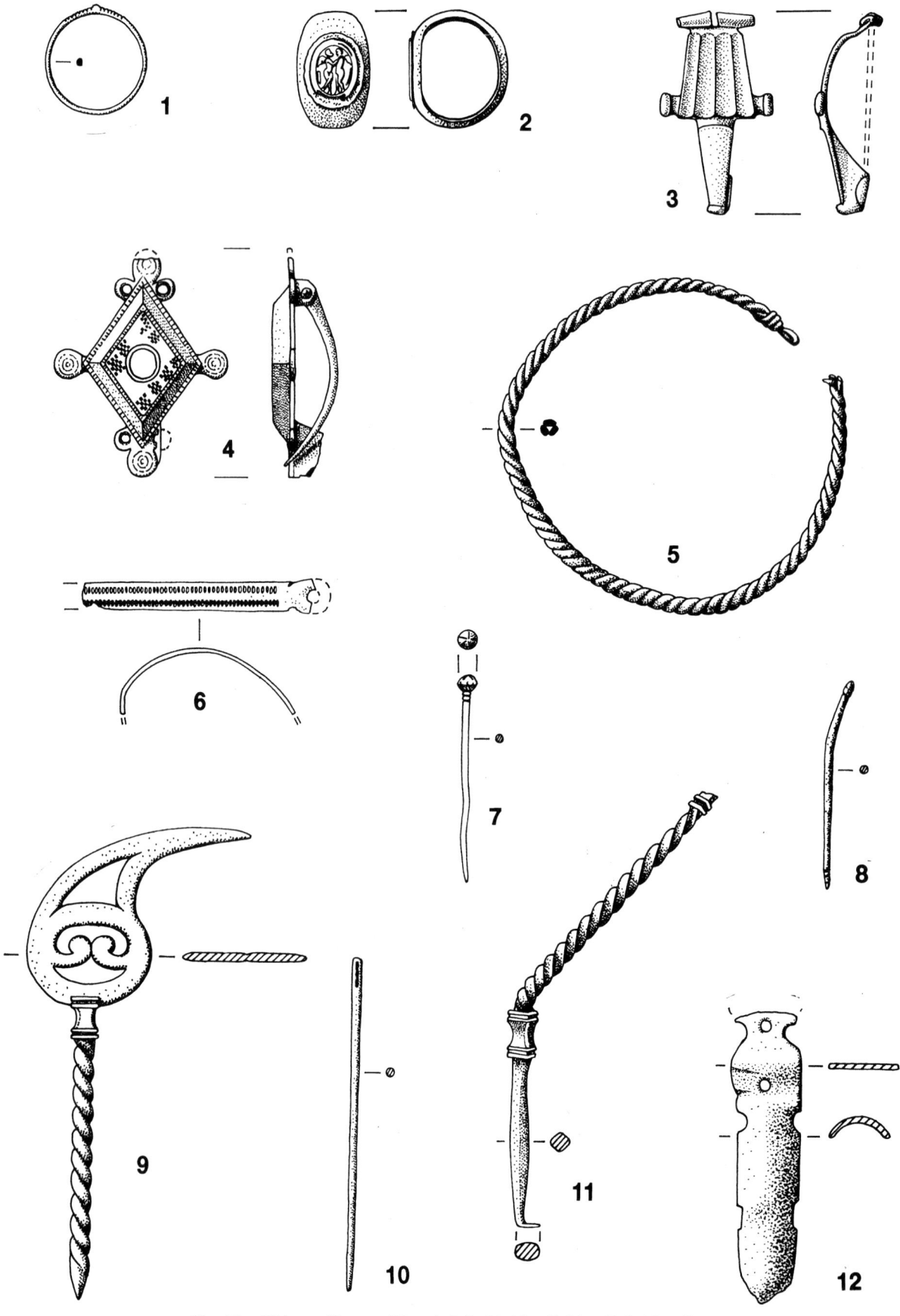

Fig. 17. Objects of bronze (Nos. 1–6, 9, 11–12 at ½: Nos. 7, 8, 10 at ½).

B. THE SMALL FINDS (NOS. 1–38)

By Keith Parfitt

Objects of Bronze

No. 1 — Simple wire finger-ring with sub-rectangular cross-section and a diameter of 17 mm. A small projection on the circumference of the ring is enclosed on either side by a zone of punched transverse grooves. Filling of Shaft F51 (ORPV–88–129).

No. 2 — Bronze ring with ribbon hoop, expanding towards bezel. Ring type XI. The bezel is set with an oval silver plate depicting in relief, Cupid and Psyche embracing. For the subject on a gilded bezel in a bronze ring, one from *Brampton, Norfolk* (Ref. 21) and note others cited. From dump over Room 15 (ORPV–88–119). Information kindly supplied by Dr. Martin Henig.

No. 3 — Brooch of Hod Hill type with projecting side-knobs at the base of the bow. The pin is missing and there are traces of a white metal coating on the upper surface. Brooches of this general type are well known in early Roman contexts on many southern British sites and may be dated to the period *c.* A.D. 40–65. Filling of Pit F62 (ORPV–88–186, KF.19).

No. 4 — Complete lozenge-shaped plate brooch with a rounded lug on each of the side-corners. A central red enamel-filled roundel is enclosed by a lozenge of dark blue enamel decorated with square panels of dots. This general form of brooch is well known on Romano-British sites but is not closely dateable. Pre-villa soil deposit (ORPV–88–9, KF.4).

No. 5 — Bracelet with a diameter of some 53 mm. made from three twisted strands of wire. A small fastening hook survives at one terminal, that at the other end being broken away. This is a very common later-Roman form of bracelet. From dump over Room 15 (ORPV–88–67).

No. 6 — Part of a bracelet made from a tapering strip of bronze. Two parallel rows of punched rectangular dots decorate the outer surface of the band. At the wider end of the fragment the punched decoration stops short of an original terminal which has a central perforation, now partially broken away. Filling of West Ditch F1 (ORPV–88–279).

No. 7 — Pin with a flattened, decorated spherical head and two horizontal grooves on the shaft below. The tapering shaft has a total length of 66 mm. The type is probably dateable to the second century A.D. Filling of the Early Terrace (ORPV–88–103).

No. 8 — Pin with a small ovoid head and single horizontal groove below. The tapering shaft, now bent, would have had an original length of some 70 mm. Three horizontal grooves have been cut into the shaft just above the tip. Filling of Late Terrace (ORPV–88–124).

No. 9 — Ornate toothpick/ear-cleaner (Ref. 22) with a pointed, comma-shaped head, of gilded bronze. The shaft has a length of 52 mm. and is spirally twisted with a decorative, squared terminal at the upper end. The comma-shaped head is decorated with a simple open-work design. Filling of West Ditch F1 (ORPV–88–27).

No. 10 — Needle of corroded bronze with a length of 117 mm. An eye, now filled with corrosion products, exists below a simple conical head. Occupation layer over Room 15 floor (ORPV–88–300).

No. 11 — Ornate *ligula* of gilded bronze, now somewhat distorted and with the upper end broken away. As surviving, the main spiral-twisted shaft is bounded by decorated, squared terminals. At the lower end a small, flat scoop is set at a right-angle to the shaft. From soils over villa (ORPV–88–13, KF.6).

No. 12 — Part of a fitting, or mount, of sheet bronze, with a generally convex cross-section. Two small holes at the upper end appear to be for attachment. Filling of Gully F81 (ORPV–88–246).

No. 13 — Upper part of a hollow rectangular handle, probably for a key. There is a suspension loop at the top surmounted by a small stud, with two horizontal grooves as decoration below. Filling of the Early Terrace. (ORPV–88–63).

No. 14 — Stud or nail with a large, flat, circular head turned down at the edges and a square-sectioned tapering shaft, 27 mm. in length. Filling of the Early Terrace (ORPV–88–7).

No. 15 — Copper alloy tweezers, broken, undecorated. Length 51 mm. Unstratified (ORPV–88–309).

Objects of Bone

No. 16 — Bone pin with hemispherical head, length 83 mm. Crummy Type 3 (Ref. 23). A.D. 200–400. From Late Terrace (ORPV–89–312).

No. 17 — Broken pin with an ovoid head and a centrally thickened shaft. Surviving length 54 mm. Crummy Type 3, broadly dateable from A.D. 200–400. Dump over Room 15 (ORPV–88–67).

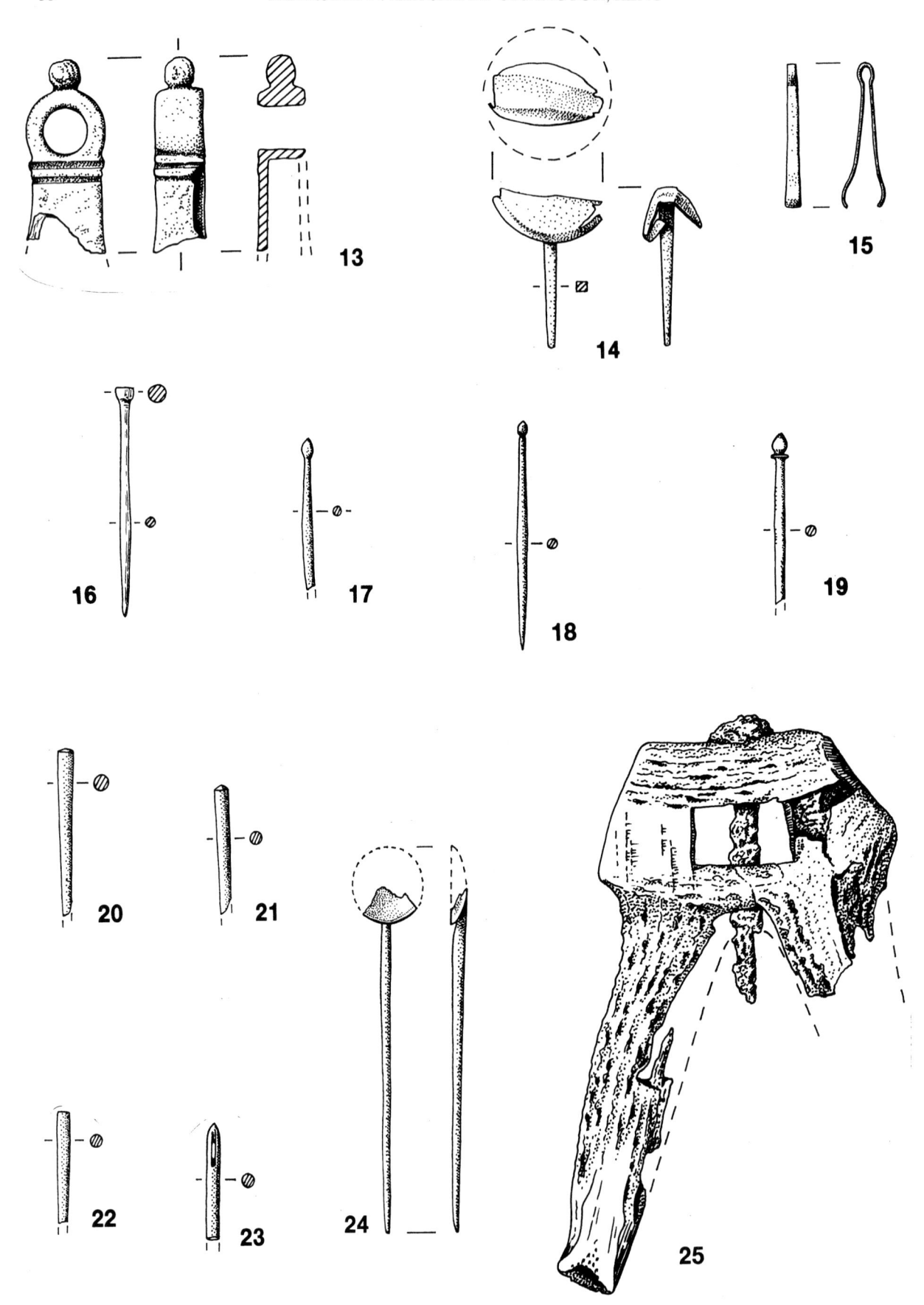

Fig. 18. Objects of bronze and bone (Nos. 13–14 at ⅟₁: Nos. 15–25 at ½).

No. 18   Complete pin with a small ovoid, faceted head and a centrally thickened shaft. Overall length 82 mm. Dump over Room 15 (ORPV–88–67).

No. 19   Broken pin with an ovoid head and a single reel below. The centrally thickened shaft is broken; the surviving overall length is 60 mm. Crummy Type 5, generally dateable to the 4th century A.D. Filling of Gully F54 (ORPV–88–255).

No. 20   Broken pin with a plain conical head and a tapering shaft. Surviving length 59 mm. Crummy Type 1, not closely dateable. From soils over villa (ORPV–88–89).

No. 21   Broken pin with a plain conical head and a tapering shaft. Surviving length 46 mm. Crummy Type 1, not closely dateable. Filling of the Early Terrace (ORPV–88–90).

No. 22   Broken pin with a simple flat head and tapering shaft. Surviving length 40 mm. Filling of the Early Terrace (ORPV–88–189).

No. 23   Broken needle with a simple conical head and a rectangular eye below. Filling of Early Terrace (ORPV–88–90).

No. 24   Broken spoon with a long tapering handle and the remains of a shallow bowl at the end. Filling of the Early Terrace (ORPV–88–74).

No. 25   Antler two-pronged rake made from the base of a red deer antler. A rectangular socket has been chiselled out to take a wooden handle. This was firmly fixed by a large iron nail (still in position) driven through the head of the rake. Damaged and worn. From Pit F107 (ORPV–89–343).

Objects of Jet and Shale

No. 26   Part of a segment of a jet bracelet with a wedge-shaped cross-section and two central perforations. The upper edge is decorated with opposed 'V' shaped notches. This type of bracelet is dateable to the late-3rd to 4th century A.D. Over clay floor in West Corridor (ORPV–88–167).

No. 27   About one third of a plain, brown shale bracelet with an estimated original diameter of about 62 mm. The cross-section of the band is oval. Filling of Period V hypocaust channel, Room 13B (ORPV–88–285).

No. 28   Part of the base of a shallow bowl or platter of brown-black shale. The vessel originally seems to have had a diameter of 440 mm. There is a small raised footring on the underside. From soils sealing villa (ORPV–88–13).

Objects of Stone

No. 29   Well worn hone of coarse, light grey sandstone, broken at one end. The object has an oval cross-section with a length of 70 mm. Filling of the Early Terrace (ORPV–88–103).

No. 30   Small chalk tablet with one flat surface containing an incised inscription along one edge (here shown at top). Function unknown though the letters are possibly inverted and the object could therefore represent a stamp. The surface, also containing an incised cross, is worn more particularly at the point of the inscription and the adjacent edge. From the Late Terrace (ORPV–88–124).

Vessels of Glass

No. 31   Vessel with a down-turned flanged rim and sloping sides of thick pale green glass. Hearth F77 (ORPV–88–66).

No. 32   Flat base fragment from a vessel of clear light blue glass. Part of an embossed letter, probably 'N', appears with a single embossed triangular shape (perhaps representing an ivy leaf) in the field above and below. Filling of the Early Terrace (ORPV–88–224).

No. 33   Straight-sided vessel with a small bead rim of clear white glass. From the West Corridor. (ORPV–88–174).

No. 34   Vessel with a flared, lobed rim of clear pale green glass. Filling of West Ditch F1 (ORPV–88–279).

No. 35   Vase or beaker with an outcurved rim and globular body decorated with applied horizontal cordons. Clear pale green glass. Filling of Shaft F51 (ORPV–88–129).

No. 36   Vessel with a flared, tubular rim of olive green glass. Packing behind hypocaust channel. Room 13B. Period V (ORPV–88–307).

No. 37   Base of ribbed 'fan-tail' handle of square or rectangular pale green opaque glass bottle. Such bottles were common from the early-Flavian period and throughout the 2nd century A.D. Dump over Room 15 (ORPV–89–313).

No. 38   Base fragment from a large vessel, with a raised footring, of pale green glass. Dump over Room 15 (ORPV–88–119).

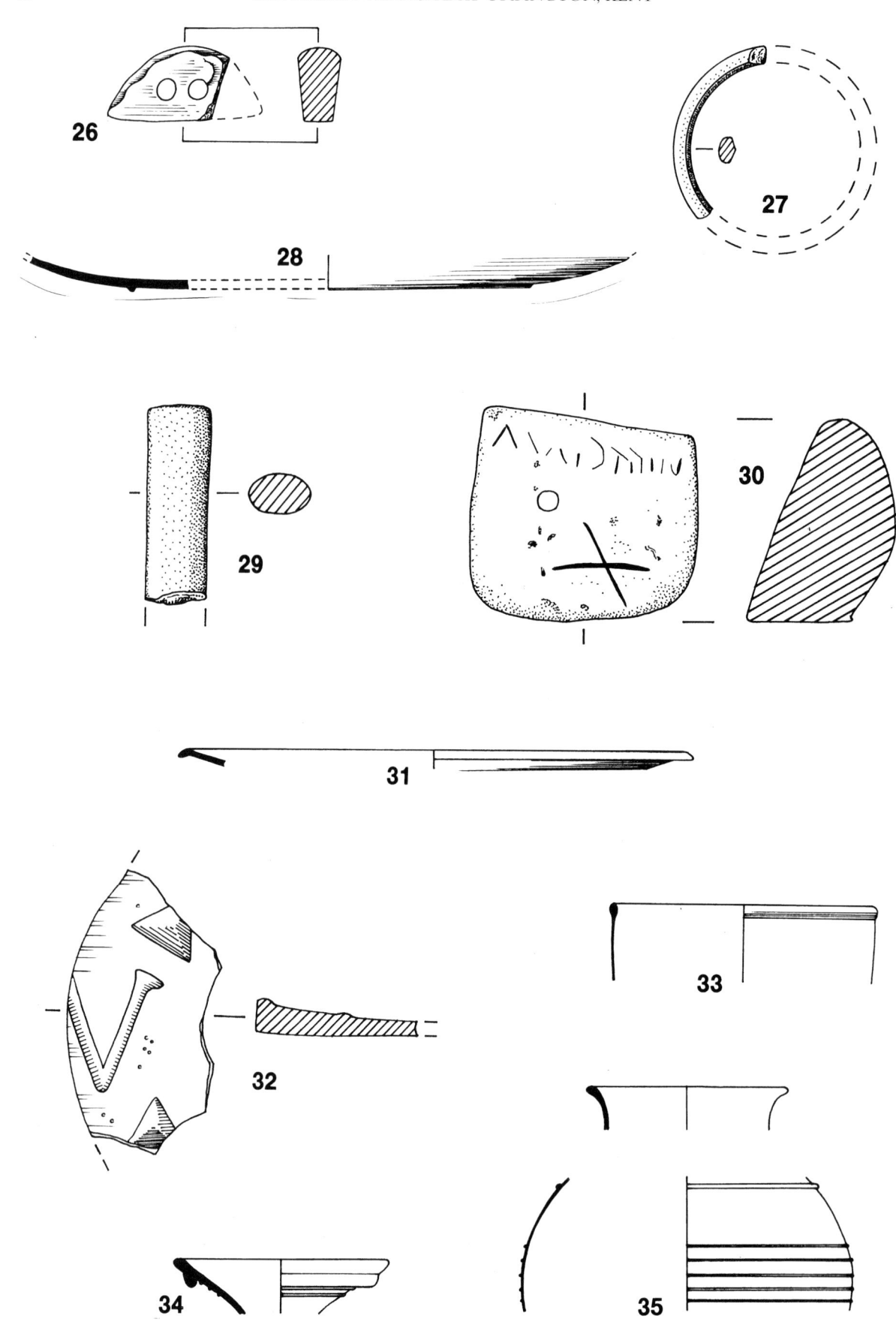

Fig. 19. Objects of Jet, shale, stone and glass (Nos. 26, 32, 34 at 1/1: Nos. 27, 29–31, 33, 35 at 1/2: No. 28 at 1/4).

THE EXCAVATED OBJECTS 61

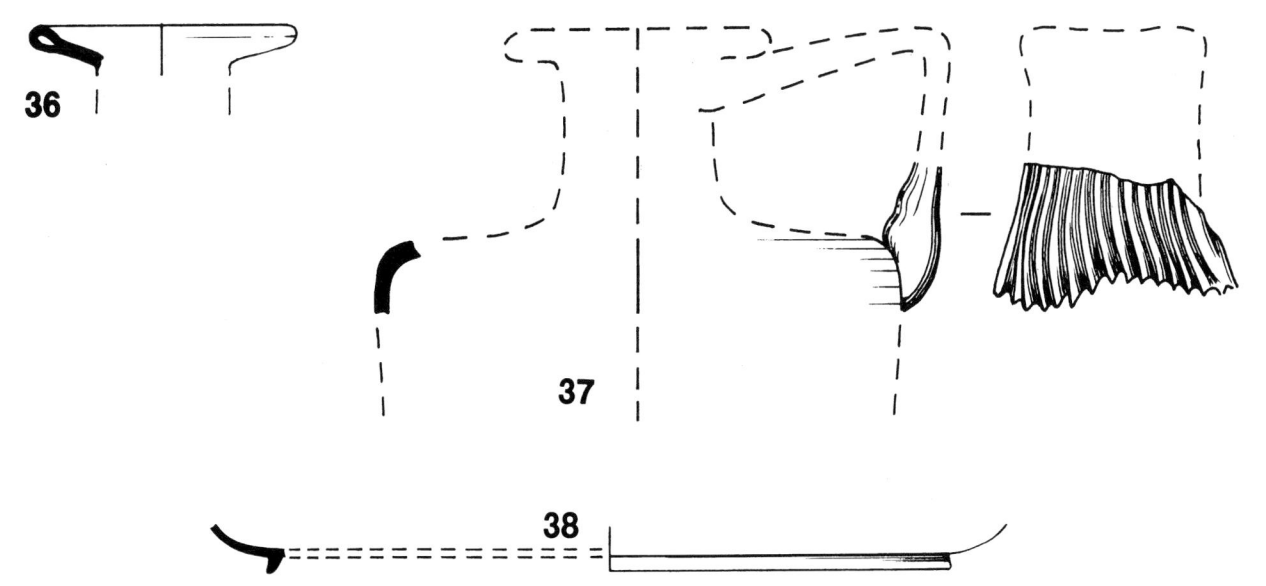

Fig. 20. Objects of glass (Nos. 36–37 at ⅟₁: No. 38 at ½).

C. THE SAMIAN WARE (NOS. 39–54)

By Joanna Bird, F.S.A.

The samian from the Crofton villa at Orpington consists of 12 decorated bowls (one of them stamped in the mould), ten plain forms with potters' stamps (not all identifiable) and sherds of a maximum of 181 other identified plain vessels. The distribution of this material by date suggests that there was little activity on the site before the middle of the 2nd century A.D. First century South Gaulish products, normally by far the most numerous on sites occupied continuously from the middle of the 1st century onwards, are few: two decorated bowls, a stamp of Aquitanus and some ten sherds of plain-ware forms. Decorated ware of the potters working in Central Gaul in the early-2nd century is entirely absent, though there are a few Central Gaulish plain-ware sherds which may date this early.

The bulk of the samian comes from Lezoux and dates from the Hadrianic-Antonine period onwards, including decorated bowls of Attianus and Criciro and a plain-ware stamp of Avitus iv. The proportion of Dr 18/31 dishes to the later Dr 31 form is 1:12, implying a considerable rise in occupation after the middle of the second century. The Antonine samian includes two decorated bowls of the Cinnamus group, one or two (one stamped) of Doeccus and one of Iullinus, and plain-ware stamps of Flo-Albinus and Genitor ii. Characteristically late-2nd century plain forms such as the mortarium Dr 45 (one example) and the Walters 79 series of dishes (two pieces) are rare, but the number of Dr 31R bowls (up to 37 sherds) shows that the higher level of samian use continued towards the end of the 2nd century.

East Gaulish products are rare, but this can reflect distribution as much as occupation. Several of the pieces, perhaps including two of the unidentified stamps, come from the Argonne and date from the Antonine period up to the turn of the 3rd century. Vessels dating definitely from the late-2nd century to the first half of the 3rd include a decorated Rheinzabern bowl, possibly by a potter of the Julius II group, a plain-ware stamp of Parentinus of Trier and perhaps the handle from a jar form.

Pre-Villa Deposits

ORPV-88-9 Dr 31, CG, Antonine
    20 Dr 30 or 37, CG, Antonine
       Dr 31, CG, Antonine (3 joining sherds)
       Dr 31, CG, Antonine
       CG sherd

West Corridor

171 (KF.14) Dr 36, CG, probably mid to later Antonine; a large example of the type. The foot is reasonably worn. (3 joined sherds; rim probably in 170, below).
    Dr 31/Lud Sb, EG, later C2-first half C3; worn inside base (4 sherds, 3 joining)
    Dr 38, EG (Trier), later C2-mid C3; burnt
    Dr 31(R), CG, Antonine

Early Terrace

  5 Dr 31, CG, Antonine
    Dr 31(R), CG, Antonine
  6 (KF 27) Dr 38 probably, CG, stamped: separate report (2 joining sherds) burnt.
    Dr 38, CG, Antonine
    2 × Dr 31, CG, Antonine
    Curle 23, CG, Antonine
    CG sherd
    Dr 33, EG (Argonne), later C2-early C3
  7 Dr 31, EG (Argonne), later C2-early C3; the slip is slightly mottled
    Dr 18, SG, Flavian

	Dr 38 probably, CG, Antonine (2 sherds)
	Dr 33, CG, Antonine
	Dr 31R, CG, mid-late Antonine (2 joining sherds)
	2 × Dr 31R, CG, mid-late Antonine
	Dr 31R, EG (Trier), later C2-C3 (2 sherds)
	CG sherd, dish form
57	2 × Dr 31, CG, Antonine
	Dr 33, CG, Antonine
	CG sherd
63	Dr 30 or 37, CG, Antonine
	2 × Dr 38, CG, Antonine
	Dr 31R, CG, mid-late Antonine (2 sherds, probably same vessel)
	3 × Dr 31 or 31R, CG, Antonine (1 burnt)
	2 × Dr 31R, CG, mid-late Antonine
	Dr 31, CG, Antonine
	Dr 31/Lud Sa, EG (Argonne), later C2-early C3 (3 sherds, including the end of the stamp)
	Lud Tb, EG, later C2-first half C3
70	Dr 33, EG (Argonne), later C2-early C3 (2 joining sherds)
	Dr 31(R), CG, Antonine
75	Dr 33, CG, Antonine
88	CG sherd, second half C2
90	Dr 18/31, CG, Hadrianic-Antonine (2 sherds)
	Dr 31, CG, mid-late Antonine; possibly overfired (4 joining sherds)
	Dr 31R, CG, mid-late Antonine; heavily burnt (2 joining sherds)
	CG sherd, Dr 31; Antonine
	CG sherd
	Late Curle 11 with deep flange and barbotine leaves; CG, Hadrianic-early Antonine (same pot as in 191 below)
	Dr 33, EG (Argonne), later C2-early C3; pale mottled slip
	EG (Argonne) sherd
103	Dr 31R, CG, mid-late Antonine
	Dr 31(R), EG (Argonne), later C2-early C3; pale mottled slip
109	Dr 31, CG, Antonine
	Dr 33, CG, Antonine
120	Dr 33, CG, Antonine
122	Dr 30 or 37, CG, Antonine
	2 CG sherds
123	Dr 37, CG, Antonine
	2 CG sherds
126	Dr 18/31, CG, Hadrianic-early Antonine
128	Dr 18/31, or 31 CG, Hadrianic-Antonine; possibly damaged in firing
189	2 × Dr 31, CG, Antonine
	Dr 33, CG, Antonine (6 joining sherds)
191	Dr 33, CG, Antonine; worn interior (joins pot in 210 below)
	Late Curle 11 with deep flange and barbotine leaves; CG, Hadrianic-early Antonine (same pot as in 90 above)
No. 39 210	Dr 33, CG, Antonine; worn interior (joins pot in 191 above)
	Dr 37 in the style of Attianus of Lezoux. The ovolo is on Stanfield & Simpson 1990, pl 85, No. 1, the beads on pl 85, No. 9, and the snake and rocks figure on pl 86, No. 12; the other animal may be a boar. Badly moulded, or perhaps damaged on removal from the mould. *c.* AD 125–150.
No. 42 224	Dr 30 in the style of Cinnamus of Lezoux. He is recorded for the trophy motif (Rogers 1974, Q43); the beads, Venus and column and the small ring are on Stanfield & Simpson 1990, pl 159, No. 34, the second Venus on pl 160, No. 35, and the astragalus and hollow terminal on pl 159, No. 26. The mask beneath the trophy is not shown by Stanfield & Simpson. The figure on the small separate sherd may be the naked man with a scarf on pl 161, No. 51. *c.* AD 150–180 (8 joined sherds and 1 small one).
	Dr 18, SG Flavian; burnt
	Dr 18/31, CG, Hadrianic (2 sherds)
	Dr 31, CG, Antonine (2 sherds)
	Dr 31(R), EG (Argonne), later C2 early C3; pale mottled slip (2 joining sherds)
	2 EG sherds (one probably Dr 33), EG (Argonne), late C2-early C3

64 THE ROMAN VILLA SITE AT ORPINGTON, KENT

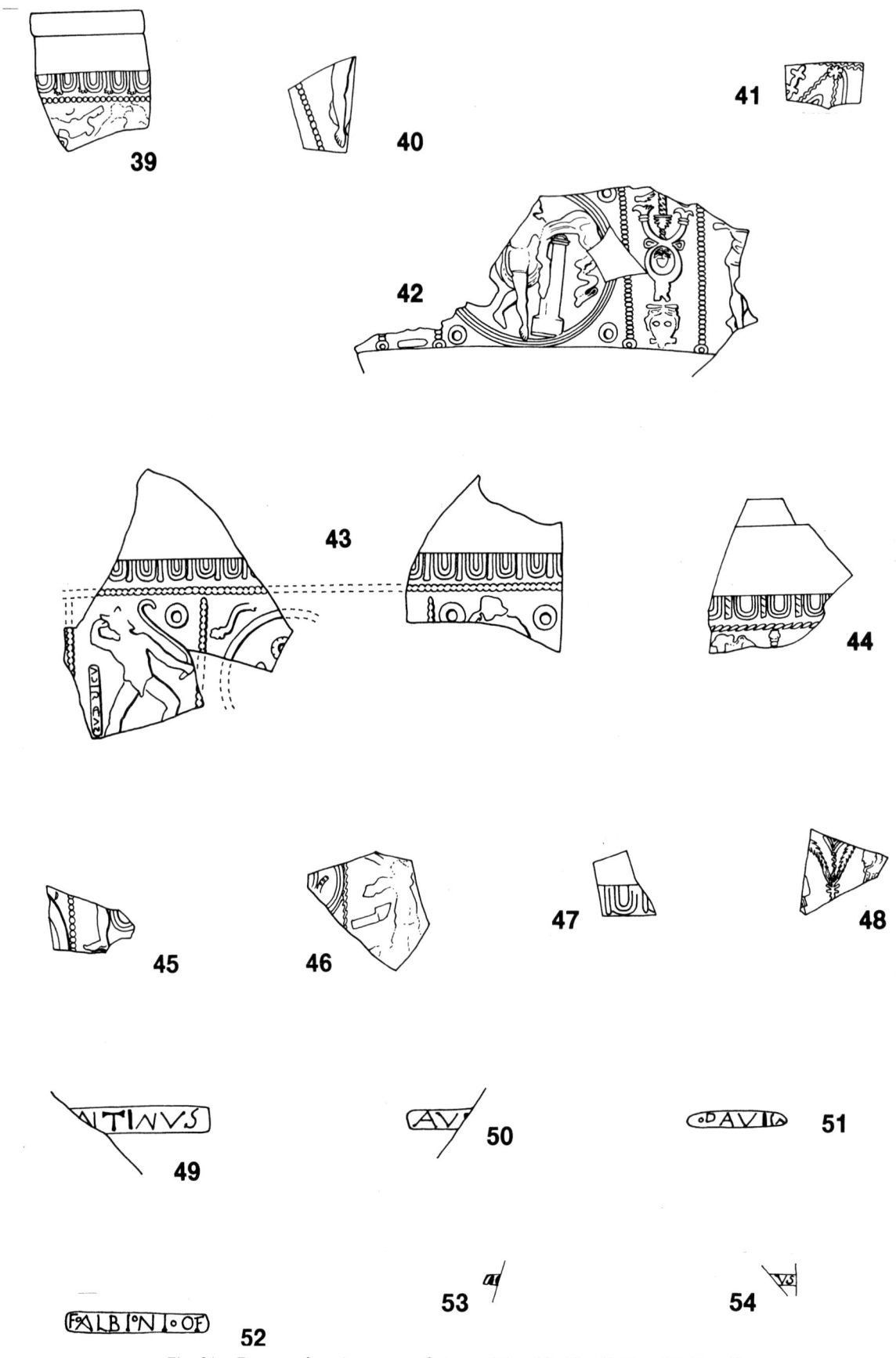

Fig. 21. Decorated samian ware and stamps (Nos. 39–48 at ½: Nos. 49–54 at ⅓).

Room 15 – Primary Occupation Layer

299 Closed form sherd, CG, Antonine probably
300 (KF 24) Dr 37 in the style of Criciro of Lezoux; same pot as 340 and 351 – see 340 below
     Dr 37 base, CG, Hadrianic-Antonine
     CG cup sherd
332 Dr 31, CG, Antonine
340 Dr 37 in the style of Criciro of Lezoux. He is recorded for this ovolo (Rogers 1974, B185); the hound is on Stanfield & Simpson 1990, pl 117, No 1, the lovers and ring terminal on pl 117, No 4, and the border on pl 118, No 17 – all signed bowls. The vine scroll is probably that on another signed bowl, with the same border and terminal: Stanfield & Simpson fig. 51, No 2. The ?animal in the festoon is not identifiable. c. A.D. 135–165. (1 sherd from 300 (KF 24), 3 sherds from 351 below).

Room 15 – Secondary Occupation Layer

331 Dr 31, CG, Antonine
351 Dr 37; three sherds from the Criciro bowl in 340 and 300 above (KF 24)
     Dr 36, CG, first half C2
     Walters 81, CG, Antonine (3 sherds); burnt.

Dump Over Room 15

No. 40 4 Dr 37, CG. The figure is probably the faun used with similar beads by Doeccus (Stanfield & Simpson, 1990, pl 149, No 31); both occur on the stamped Doeccus bowl from 13 below. It is not possible to identify this sherd as definitely the same bowl, as the heavy wear noted on the other pieces is absent here. Mid-late Antonine.
     (KF 25) Dr 31, EG, stamped: separate report]SI[?Argonne; later C2-early C3
     Dr 40, CG, Antonine; worn interior (2 joining sherds)
     Dr 33, CG, Antonine
67   Lud Sb, EG, (Rheinzabern), late C2-mid C3 (2 joining sherds)
     Dr 33, EG, later C2-first half C3
     Dr 38, CG, Antonine (3 joining sherds)
     Dr 31, CG, Antonine
     CG dish/bowl sherd
119 Dr 37, CG, Hadrianic-Antonine
     Dr 33, CG, Antonine (2 joining sherds)
     Dr 33, EG, later C2-first half C3 (2 joining sherds)
     EG sherd, possibly slightly burnt
313 Dr 31R, CG, mid-later Antonine (5 joining sherds, 1 other rim)
     Dr 31(R), CG, Antonine
     2 CG sherds, Dr 31(R)
     Dr 33, CG, Antonine
317 Dr 37 in the style of the Cinnamus group at Lezoux. The ovolo, fine beads, bird and similar scrollery are on Stanfield & Simpson 1990, pl 162, No 59. c. A.D. 145–175
     Dr 36, SG, Flavian
     Dr 31, CG, Antonine
     CG sherd
329 Dr 36, CG, Hadrianic-Antonine (2 joining sherds)

Pit F62

178 Dr 33, CG, Antonine
     CG sherd
179 Dr 33, CG, Antonine
     CG sherd, probably Dr 31 and Antonine
187 Dr 27, SG, early-mid Flavian
215 Dr 15/17, SG, pre- or early Flavian

Room 14C (Behind Plaster)

347 Dr 31, CG, Antonine

Middle Terrace (Period IV)

    323 Dr 36, CG, Hadrianic-Antonine (joins dish in 329 above)
          Dr 31R, CG, mid-late Antonine
    324 (KF 31) Dr 31, CG, stamped: separate report
    325 Dr 33, CG, Antonine

Room 14D

    96 Dr 33, CG, Hadrianic-Antonine
    183 Dr 31, CG, Antonine
    185 Dr 27, CG, Hadrianic-early Antonine, and probably at the later end of the range
    296 Dr 33, EG, (Rheinzabern probably), later C2-mid C3
    302 Dr 33, CG, Antonine
    334 Dr 18/31, Hadrianic-Antonine

Late Terrace

    124 CG sherd, Hadrianic-Antonine
    158 Dr 33, CG, Antonine; slightly burnt
          Dr 31, CG, Antonine; burnt
    182 Dr 18, SG, Flavian
          CG sherd, probably Dr 31 and Antonine

Late Ditch (F1)

    10 CG sherd, second half C2
    12 Dish, CG, second half C2; heavily worn interior (2 joining sherds)
    23 Dr 31, CG, Antonine
    26 Dr 37 in the style of Doeccus of Lezoux (joins KF 7, 13 below)
          CG sherd
    59 CG sherd, second half C2
    175 Dr 31, CG, Antonine
    207 Dr 37, CG, Antonine

Final Soil Deposits

    3 Dr 33, CG, Antonine
    8 Dr 33, CG, Antonine

No. 43 13 (KF 7) Dr 37 with mould stamp of Doeccus of Lezoux (separate report). The ovolo, beads and stamp are on Stanfield & Simpson 1990, pl 147, No 1, the faun on pl 149, No 31, the beaded circle on pl 149, No 28, and the horn motif on pl 151, No 58. The other figure is the naked man with scarf on pl 148, No 22. Doeccus normally used double medallions, and it is possible that the motif here is an arcade, using the scroll element on pl 147, No 7. *c.* A.D. 165–200. (3 sherds, 2 of them joining and joining the sherd from 26 above; 1 sherd from 89 below; possible further sherd from 4 above)

No. 44   Dr 37 in the style of Iullinus of Lezous. Ovolo, corded border and vertical bead-and-reel border, as Stanfield and Simpson 1990, pl 125, No 1; the figure is the Venus on pl 127, No 31. *c.* A.D. 160–190.

No. 52   (KF 8)Dr 33, CG, stamped: separate report ALBINI.OF Trajanic-Hadrianic
        2 × Dr 33. CG, Antonine
        Dr 31R/Lud Sb, EG, later C2-early C3
        Dr 31R, CG, mid-later Antonine

No. 46 60 Dr 37, CG. Panel of shallow wavy lines with a double medallion; the figure is too abraded to identify certainly (? a cupid). The slip and very micaceous fabric suggest a Hadrianic date.
        2 × Dr 33, CG, Antonine
        CG sherd, second half C2

No. 45 89 Dr 37: sherd from stamped Doeccus bowl (KF 7, see 13 above)
        Dr 33, CG, Antonine (2 joining sherds)
        Dr 33, SG, Flavian-Trajanic
        Dr 31, CG, Antonine
        3 CG sherds, Dr 31, Antonine
        CG sherd
        144 Dr 33, CG, Antonine

No. 49 170 (KF17) Dr 31, EG, stamped: separate report (2 joining sherds)]NTI/VVS, later C2-first half C3.
Dr 36, CG, probably mid to later Antonine, and probably the rim of KF 14 in 171 above (3 sherds)
Dr 38, EG, late C2-mid C3; worn (2 joining sherds)
Dr 31(R), CG, Antonine (2 joining sherds)
Dr 31(R), CG, Antonine
Burnt CG sherd, probably Dr 31 or 31R
Round-sectioned handle from a small flagon or jar, EG, later C2-first half C3
209 Dr 31(R), CG, Antonine
213 Dr 31R, CG, mid-later Antonine
225 Walters 79 etc, CG, mid-later Antonine
263 Sherd, closed form, CG, Antonine
310 Dr 37, CG: part of small boar, probably, in freestyle arrangement; Antonine
Dr 45, CG, later C2
Base and rim, Dr 31R, CG, mid-late Antonine (2 vessels)
Dr 33, CG, Antonine
CG sherd

Pits and Post-Holes
No. 54 30 (KF.26) Dr 31, CG, stamped: separate report] VS[Probably Antonine (F-9).
No. 41 Dr 37, SG, Panel design, including saltire with formal bud. *c.* A.D. 70–85 (F-9)
78 Dr 31, CG, Antonine (F-48)
52 Dr 31R, CG, mid-later Antonine (F-40)
156 2 × Dr 31(R), CG, Antonine (F-95)
342 Dr 36, CG, Hadrianic-early Antonine (2 sherds) (F-107)
343 Dr 18/31, CG, Hadrianic-early Antonine (F-107)
No. 50 79 (KF 9) Dr 31, CG, stamped; separate report AV![Probably Antonine (F-27)

Miscellaneous Ditches
168 CG sherd, probably Dr 31(R); Antonine (F-54)
246 Dr 31, CG, Antonine (F-81)
262 CG sherd, probably Dr 31, second half C2 (F-86)

Unstratified
1 Dr 33, CG, Antonine (3 sherds, probably one vessel)
Dr 38, EG, later C2-mid C3
Dr 33, EG, later C2-mid C3
Dr 31 base, EG, later C2-mid C3; possibly slightly burnt
Dr 38 probably, CG, Antonine; slightly burnt
2 sherds, Dr 31R, CG, mid-late Antonine; probably two vessels
Bowl, CG, later C2; slip completely lost on interior
2 2 × Dr 33, CG, Antonine
32 Dr 31(R), CG, Antonine
2 bowl/dish sherds, CG, Hadrianic-Antonine; possibly same vessel
40 Dr 31R, CG, mid-late Antonine (3 sherds, one of them burnt; probably one vessel)
Dr 31(R), CG, Antonine
Lud Sb, EG, late C2-mid C3
CG sherd
No. 48 Dr 30, SG. Arcade of wreaths balanced on vertical wavy-lines, with a repeated figure of Penelope. Hermet 1934, pl 73, shows a number of similar bowls: No 2 has a similar wreath, No 8 has what may be the same leaf at the top of the vertical and Nos 13–14 have figures of Penelope. *c.* A.D. 50–65
No. 47 Dr 37, Rheinzabern. The ovolo, Ricken & Fischer 1963, E23, was shared by a number of potters, but the late ware of this sherd suggests a potter of The Julius II group. Early-mid C3
83 Dr 31, CG, Antonine
No. 51 245 Dr 27, SG, stamped: separate report (KF 20) Probably Neronian
Dr 33, CG, Antonine
Base, Walters 79 etc., CG, mid-later Antonine (2 joining sherds)
Dr 31/Lud Sa, EG, later C2-first half C3

253   SG platter base sherd, second half C1
311   (KF 32) Dr 31, CG, stamped: separate report, Antonine
      Dr 36, CG, first half C2
      SG bowl base, second half C1
      Dr 33, CG, Antonine
      Dr 31(R), CG, Antonine

References

Hermet, See Ref. 24.
Ricken and Fischer, See Ref. 25.
Rogers, See Ref. 26.
Stanfield & Simpson, See Ref. 27.

D. POTTERS' STAMPS ON SAMIAN WARE

By Brenda Dickinson

Each entry gives: excavation number, potter (i, ii, etc., where homonyms are involved), die number, form, reading of the stamp, published example, pottery of origin, date.

(a) and (b) indicates

(a) Stamp attested at the pottery in question.

(b) Potter, but not the particular stamp, attested at the pottery in question. Ligatured letters are underlined.

No. 49 (1)   (KF17) Parentinus 2d on form Lud. Sa or Sb [PARE]NTINVS Trier (a). There is no site dating evidence for this stamp, but one from another die comes from Niederbieber and will not be earlier than c. A.D. 180/190. Parentinus's use of forms 31R and 32 also suggests activity in the late-second or first half of the third century. (ORPV–8–170).

No. 50 (2)   (KF9) Avitus iv 7a on form 31 AVI[TVSF] (Curle 1911, 236, no. 6). Lezoux (b). Avitus iv almost certainly began work under Hadrian, but his plain ware is common in Antonine Scotland. This particular stamp is known from Bar Hill (2), Camelon (2), Inveresk and Newstead (4). c. A.D. 130–150. (ORPV–88–79).

No. 51 (3)   (KF20) Aquitanus Ic' on form 27g OFAQVITAN(from a die originally giving OFAQVITANI) (Ulbert 1969, Taf. 9, 10) La Graufesenque (a). Aquitanus's stamps occasionally appear on form Ritterling 5, and so he can scarcely have started work later than c. A.D. 40. However, this particular stamp is not associated with the form and is likely to be slightly later. The potter's career continued down to A.D. 60 or beyond, and his stamps occur in the pottery shops at Colchester destroyed in A.D. 60/61, c. A.D. 45–65. (ORPV–88–245).

No. 52 (4)   (KF8) Flo-Albinus 4a on form 33 F·ALBINI· OF Lezoux (b). This potter, whose precise name is not clear from his stamps, stamped the rims of decorated bowls in the styles of Cinnamus ii and the Paternus v group. His plain forms include the later-second century dish, form 31R, c. A.D. 150–180. (ORPV–88–13).

No. 53 (5)   (KF25)]SIC[? on form 31, perhaps East Gaulish (Argonne?). Antonine? (ORPV–88–4).

No. 54 (6)   (KF26)]VS[on form 31, Central Gaulish. Antonine. (ORPV–88–30)

       (7)   (KF31) Genitor ii 5b on form 31 G[ENITORF] Lezoux (a). This stamp occurs in a pottery store at Corbridge, with stamped vessels of mid-to late-Antonine date (Forster 1908, 270, fig. 10, with 247–58). It is also known from Chesterholm and was used on forms 31R and 79. c. A.D. 160–200. (ORPV–89–324).

No. 43 (8)   (KF7) Do(v)eccus i 13a on form 37 DOIICCVS retr. (S. & S. 1958, pl. 147, 2) Lezoux (b). A stamp of one of the latest Lezoux potters to export to Britain. It is known from Benwell, Haltonchesters (2) and Wallsend and occurs in late-Antonine burials at Brougham. c. 165–200. (ORPV–88–13, 26, 89).

       (9)   (KF27) Illegible stamp on form 38, Central Gaulish. Antonine. (ORPV–88–6).

      (10)   (KF32]IIC[on form 31, Central Gaulish. Antonine. (ORPV–89–311).

      (11)   DE[? on form 31, perhaps East Gaulish (Argonne?). Antonine. (ORPV–88–63).

References

Curle, See Ref. 28.
Forster, See Ref. 29.
S. & S. See Ref. 30.
Ulbert, See Ref. 31.

E. THE MORTARIA (NOS. 55–71)

By Kay Hartley

Seventeen selected mortaria from the site were sent to me for examination. Of these, eight are from the Oxford potteries and date between A.D. 240–400; six dating within the period A.D. 120–250 are likely to be from local sources in Kent, though Colchester would not be impossible for some of these. Two second century mortaria are from potteries in the Verulamium region and at Much Hadham. The single import, from the Rhineland, is dated A.D. 150–300. Each vessel is described below.

No. 55.   ORPV88-9 (Pre-Villa Deposits). Dr. 24 cms. Fine-textured, micaceous, creamy brown fabric; rare, ill-sorted, quartz with opaque white and black inclusions. No trituration grit survives but it was probably flint and quartz. Self-coloured. In form and to a large extent in fabric, this mortarium is in the Colchester/Kent, second-century tradition and would best fit a date within the period A.D. 120–160. The very soapy texture of the fabric is, however, alien to the known potteries in Kent, Essex and Wiggonholt, which produced such mortaria. It is most likely to be from a very local source.

No. 56.   ORPV88-10 (West Ditch F1). Dr. 45 cms. Almost brownish-cream fabric with slightly sandy texture; moderate, ill-sorted, quartz and opaque orange-brown inclusions; trituration grit consisted of abundant, well-sorted, sub-rounded quartz, mostly pinkish in colour but including transparent and milky shades. A typical mortarium from the Oxford potteries of Young 1977, type M22.19 dated A.D. 240–400. It has, however, traces of matt red-brown slip on the spout and in the grooves on the bead and flange. Young does not record any example of this form with such a colour-coat so that it is an unusual feature.

No. 57.   ORPV88-12 (West Ditch F1). Dr. 18 cms. Fine-textured, micaceous, orange-brown fabric; rare, quartz and opaque orange-brown inclusions. Slight traces of the orange-brown colour-coat survive. Trituration grit as No. 56. An incomplete rim-fragment from a typical wall-sided mortarium from the Oxford potteries, Young type C97, dated A.D. 240–400.

No. 58.   ORPV88-26 (West Ditch F.1). Dr. 18 cms. Incomplete rim-fragment, identical in form, fabric, and date to no. 57; from the same or a similar vessel.

No. 59.   ORPV88-58 (West Ditch F.1). Dr. 37 cms. Fabric generally similar to no. 56 with more inclusions and a thick deep pink core. Oxford potteries, type Young 22, dated A.D. 240–400. This mortarium is normal in that it does not have a colour-coat.

No. 60.   ORPV88-246 (Ditch F.81). Dr. 20 cms. Fine-textured cream fabric with few tiny quartz and flint inclusions visible; self-coloured. No trituration grit survives. The fabric would fit with production in Kent (possibly at Canterbury), or at Colchester. This exact rim-form could probably be matched in both areas *c.* A.D. 190–250 but very small mortaria in this date range are noticeably more common in Kent, suggesting origin there. Heavily worn.

No. 61.   ORPV88-156 (Pit F.95). Dr. 31 cms. Hard, fine-textured, reddish-brown fabric merging into the thick grey core; few tiny quartz and red-brown inclusions; cream slip; trituration grit mostly quartz with hackly fracture, some flint, rare ?haematite. Collared mortarium similar in form and perhaps in fabric to Bennett, Frere and Stow 1982 fig. 84, no. 2 (text wrongly placed under 156, fig. 84, no. 1). Probably made in Kent. This rim-profile was produced in the Rhineland *c.* A.D. 150–300 but the optimum date for production in Kent would have been A.D. 170–250. Well-worn.

No. 62.   ORPV88-215 (Pit F.62). Dr. 27 cms. Fabric generally similar to nos. 56 and 59. Oxford potteries. Young type M18. A.D. 240–300.

No. 63.   ORPV88-259 (Pit F.87). Incomplete rim-section in drab cream fabric with fairly frequent, ill-sorted quartz inclusions; one large quartz trituration grit survives. Typical of mortaria made in the Verulamium region A.D. 140–180.

No. 64.   ORPV88-123 (Early Terrace). Dr. 26 cms. Drab cream fabric of crumbly texture with fairly frequent, ill-sorted quartz inclusions; trituration grit mostly if not entirely tiny quartz over the whole interior. Typical of mortaria made in the Rhineland A.D. 140–300 (Holbrook and Bidwell 1991, Types TC56–58, 205–7). Worn and slightly burnt.

No. 65.   ORPV88-167 (West Corridor). Dr. 29 cms. Fabric generally similar to nos. 56, 59 and 62. Oxford potteries, Young type M18. A.D. 240–300. Worn.

No. 66.   ORPV88-3 (Soils over Villa). Fine-textured, brownish-cream fabric with sparse, ill-sorted quartz inclusions. Self-coloured. A fragment from the collar of a wall-sided mortarium of Hull type 501 (Hull 1963), with two

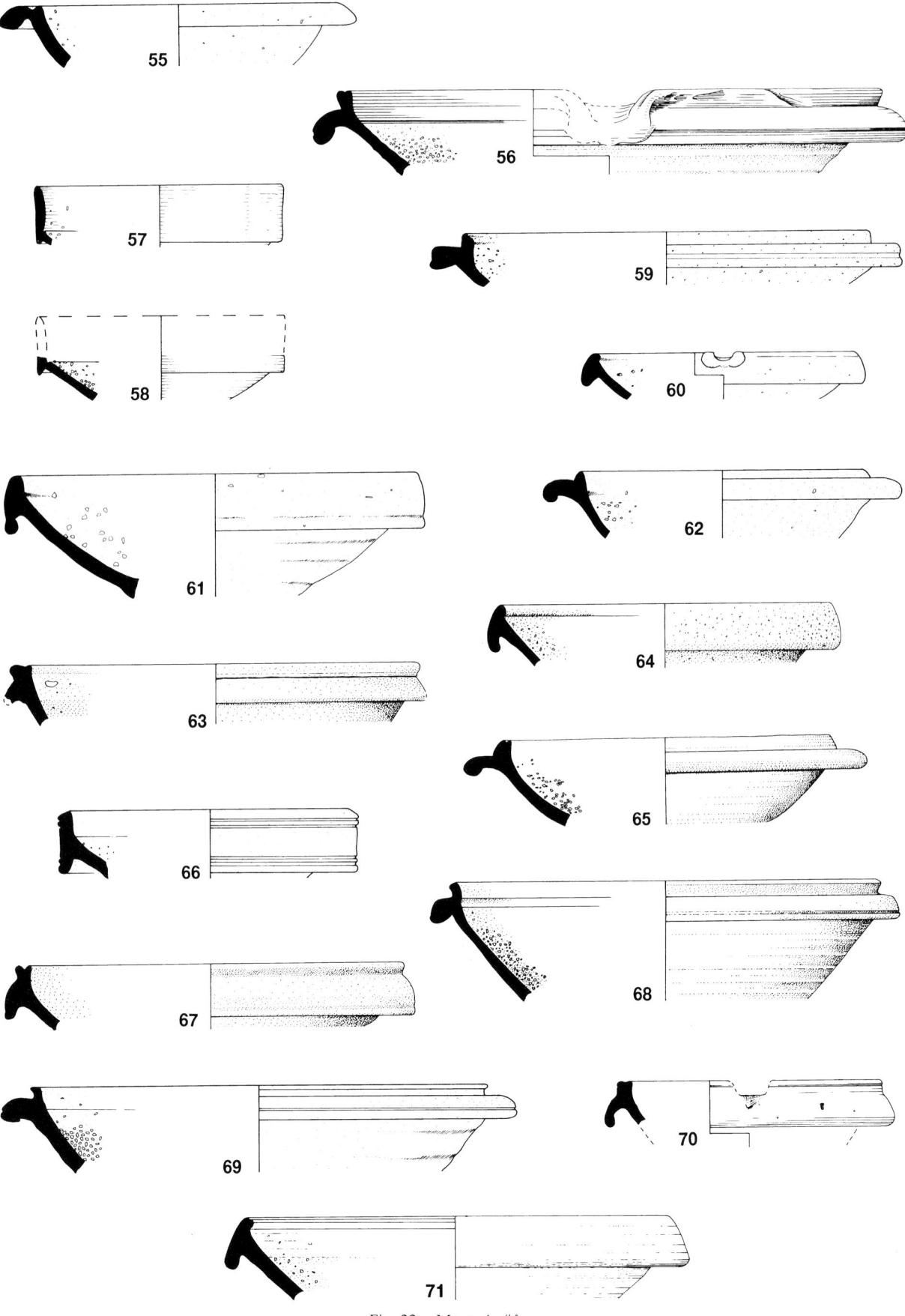

Fig. 22.   Mortaria (¼)

grooves at top and bottom. This is likely to be from an unstamped example of this type, made at Colchester and in Kent (probably Canterbury). *c.* A.D. 180–230+. Slightly burnt.

No. 67. ORPV88–13 (Soils over Villa). Dr. 30 cms. The fabric is slightly abrasive and the clearly defined grey core is uniformly thick throughout leaving about 2 mm thickness of orange-brown colour at all surfaces; moderate to fairly frequent ill-sorted quartz with rare, large red-brown inclusions. Self-coloured. No trituration grit survives. This rim-profile is of a type primarily made in the Verulamium region A.D. 140–180+ (Frere 1972, no. 1425, 1983, no. 1425, and 1984, no. 2682 and *passim* in all vols.), but this fabric can be attributed either to the potteries at Much Hadham or to some local source working in the same tradition. Slightly burnt.

No. 68. ORPV88–134 (Shaft F.51). Dr. 30 cms. Hard, fine-textured, orange-brown fabric with grey core in parts; few tiny quartz and rare large red-brown inclusions; this example includes a large calcareous inclusion. Cream slip. Trituration grit identical with that in nos. 56–59 etc. Oxford potteries. Young form WC7. A.D. 240–400.

No. 69. ORPV88–147 (Shaft F.58). Dr. 44 cms. Fabric and trituration grit as nos. 56, 59 and 62. Oxford potteries. Young form M18. A.D. 240–300.

No. 70. ORPV88–146 (Shaft F.58). Dr. 23 cms. Fine-textured, red-brown fabric merging to thick brown core with moderate, ill-sorted quartz and fewer opaque black inclusions; no trituration grit survives. Cream slip. *c.* A.D. 160–220. Probably local. Worn.

No. 71. ORPV89–328 (Middle Terrace). Dr. 30 cms. Fabric as no. 66; the trituration grit consists of flint, quartz and occasional calcareous material. A collared mortarium of exactly the kind made in the Rhineland A.D. 150–300 but in a fabric made probably in Kent rather than Colchester. The most likely date for manufacture in Kent is probably within the period A.D. 170–250.

References

Bennett et al 1982. See Ref. 32
Frere 1972 See Ref. 33
Frere 1983 See Ref. 34
Frere 1984 See Ref. 35
Holbrook 1991 See Ref. 36
Hull 1963 See Ref. 37
Young 1977 See Ref. 38

F. THE COARSE POTTERY (NOS. 72–175)

By Peter Keller AIFA

About 10,000 pieces of pottery, almost exclusively Roman, were recovered from the site during the 1988–9 excavations. These included 298 sherds of samian ware and perhaps 50 sherds of mortaria, mostly reported above. Of the coarse pottery little came from the villa rooms, which had mostly been cleared during earlier work. Most came from the terraces behind the villa, or from over 100 features, whilst some 1,400 sherds were effectively unstratified.

Whilst the coarse pottery has been subjected to a preliminary examination, lack of substantial resources has precluded a detailed fabric analysis. The following catalogue deals mainly with the dating evidence, in keeping with current selectivity, now widely adopted in archaeological reports. The catalogue contains illustrations and descriptions of 104 pottery vessels. These have been assigned broad dates based on the typology of pottery from West Kent sites and Kent sites in general (summarised in Pollard 1988). Where applicable, parallels have been quoted from sites in East and West Kent where similar vessels occur, in order to support the general dates proposed. The sources have been abbreviated and a list is included below.

Early Ditch (F59 and F101)

No. 72 Small cooking pot with thickened rim of red-brown sandy ware with dark grey surfaces. Compares with WK 262 dated A.D. 80–130. (ORPV–88–247).

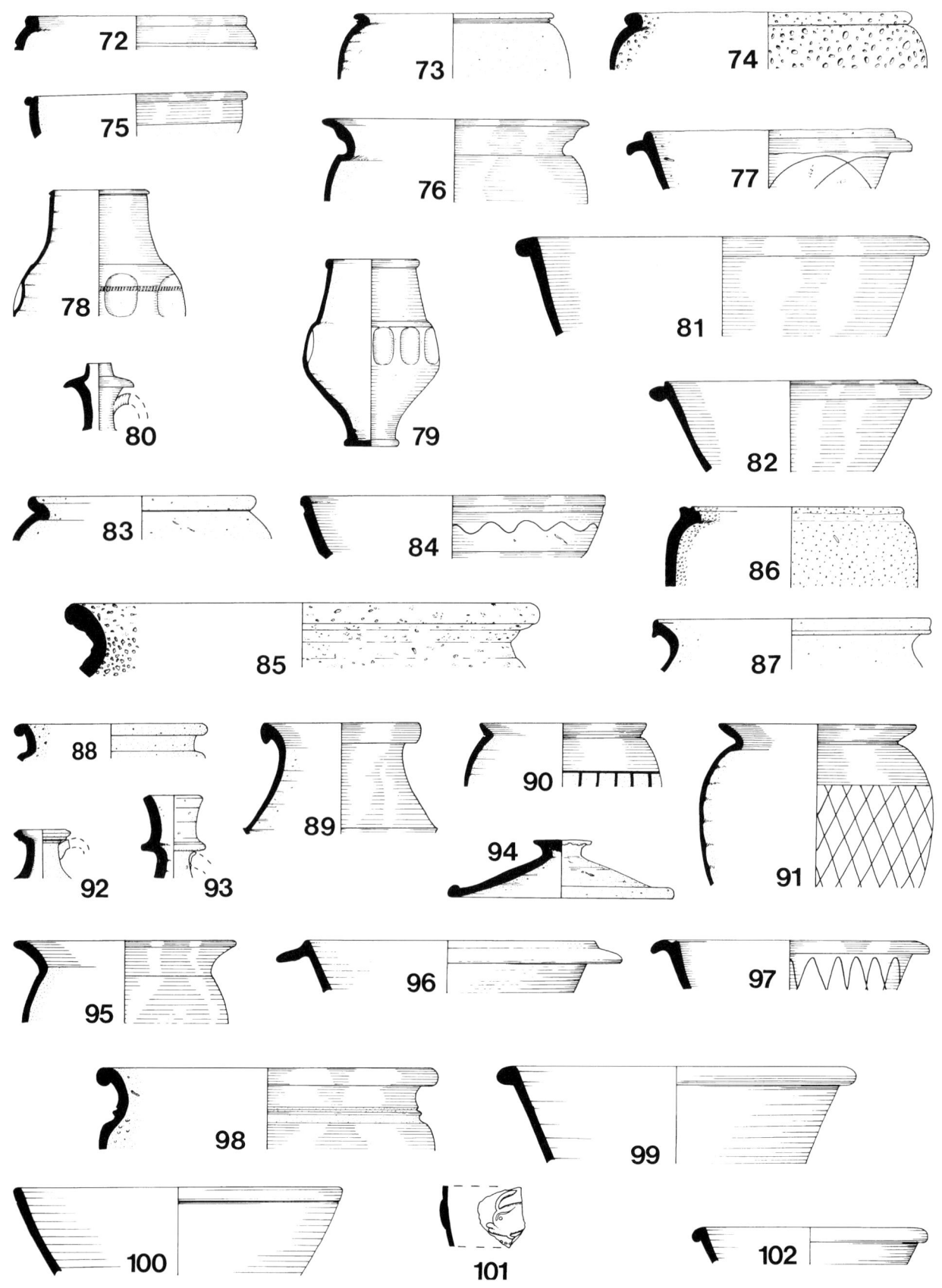

Fig. 23. Coarse pottery (¼).

Pre-Villa Deposits

No. 73　Vessel with flattened bead rim of light grey sandy ware with grey surfaces. Compare with Mon. 3F6.1. A.D. 80–150. (ORPV–88–107).

No. 74　Cooking pot with bead rim of grey 'corky' ware with mottled grey-brown surfaces. Common amongst the shell-tempered wares in West Kent during the first and early-second centuries AD. Compare WK 200 and KES–1 288. (ORPV–88–121).

No. 75　Dish with bead rim of dark grey sandy ware with dark grey to black exterior and orange-brown interior surface. A.D. 60–120. (ORPV–88–284).

West Corridor

No. 76　Jar with cavetto rim of BB2 ware. Burnished exterior to inside of rim. A.D. 180–220. (ORPV–88–171).

No. 77　Flanged dish of dark grey to black sandy ware. Compares KES–1 841. Common form during the period A.D. 250–350. (ORPV–88–171).

No. 78　Beaker of Rhenish ware with brown, metallic high gloss, surfaces. A.D. 180–220. (ORPV–88–171).

No. 79　Indented beaker of colour-coat ware with red-brown high lustre surfaces. Compare KES–1 763. A.D. 250–300. (ORPV–88–171).

No. 80　Flagon with flanged neck of orange-buff sandy (colour-coat) ware. A.D. 250–300. (ORPV–88–171).

No. 81　Dish with bead rim of grey sandy NKM/TS ware. As MON.5C1. A.D. 180–220. (Beam slot F.82, slot by wall). (ORPV–88–252)

No. 82　Flanged bowl of grey sandy NKM/TS ware with grey-brown surfaces. As MON.5A4. A.D. 200–250. (Beam-slot F.75). (ORPV–88–253)

Early Terrace

No. 83　Cooking pot with recessed rim of dark grey coarse sandy ware with mottled grey-brown surfaces. Early-second century A.D. (ORPV–88–6)

No. 84　Dish with upright grooved rim of BB2 ware. Late-second century A.D. (ORPV–88–6).

No. 85　Storage jar with outcurved rim of Patch Grove ware with buff-brown surfaces. Common in West Kent during late-first to mid-second century A.D. (ORPV–88–7).

No. 86　Cooking pot with recessed bead rim of Patch Grove ware with buff to buff-brown surfaces. Early-second century A.D. (ORPV–88–7)

No. 87　Cooking pot with squared rim of dark red-brown sandy NKM/TS ware with orange-brown surfaces. Compare with MON.3H5.3. A.D. 180–230. (ORPV–88–75).

No. 88　Jar with rolled rim of red-brown sandy NKM/TS ware with light grey surfaces. Second century A.D. (ORPV–88–88).

No. 89　Jar with thickened rim of light-grey sandy Highgate Wood type ware with grey-brown surfaces. Compare WK.375. Second century A.D. (ORPV–88–90)

No. 90　Jar with everted rim of grey sandy NKM/TS ware. Compare MON.2H. A.D. 80–150. (ORPV–88–90).

No. 91　Jar with everted rim of grey sandy NKM/TS ware. MON.3J(1/0). Late-second century A.D. (ORPV–88–90).

No. 92　Small flagon rim and neck, of orange-red fine sandy ware with all-over cream-white slip. Compare DOV–1 558 of second century A.D. date. (ORPV–88–123).

No. 93　Large flagon or bottle of cream to buff fine sandy ware. Probably mid to late-second century A.D. (ORPV–88–189).

No. 94　Lid of light grey sandy NKM/TS ware with buff-brown surfaces. Compare MON.12C and DOV-2 157, early-second century A.D. (ORPV–88–210).

Dump over Room 15

No. 95　Jar with cavetto rim of Alice Holt type ware with silver-grey surfaces. Compare AH/F Class 3b. Mid-second to third century A.D. (ORPV–88–4).

No. 96　Dish with broad flange of grey sandy ware with grey to black surfaces. First half of third century A.D. (ORPV–88–4).

No. 97　Dish with flanged rim of grey sandy NKM/TS ware. Compare MON.5B3.1. First half of third century A.D. (ORPV–88–67)

No. 98　Large jar with thickened outcurved rim of orange-brown sandy ware with dark grey burnished exterior surface to inside of rim. Compare DOV–1 470. First half of second century A.D. (ORPV–88–67).

No. 99　Dish with bead rim of dark grey sandy ware with silver-grey to brown surfaces. Common during the period A.D. 180–220. (ORPV–88–119).

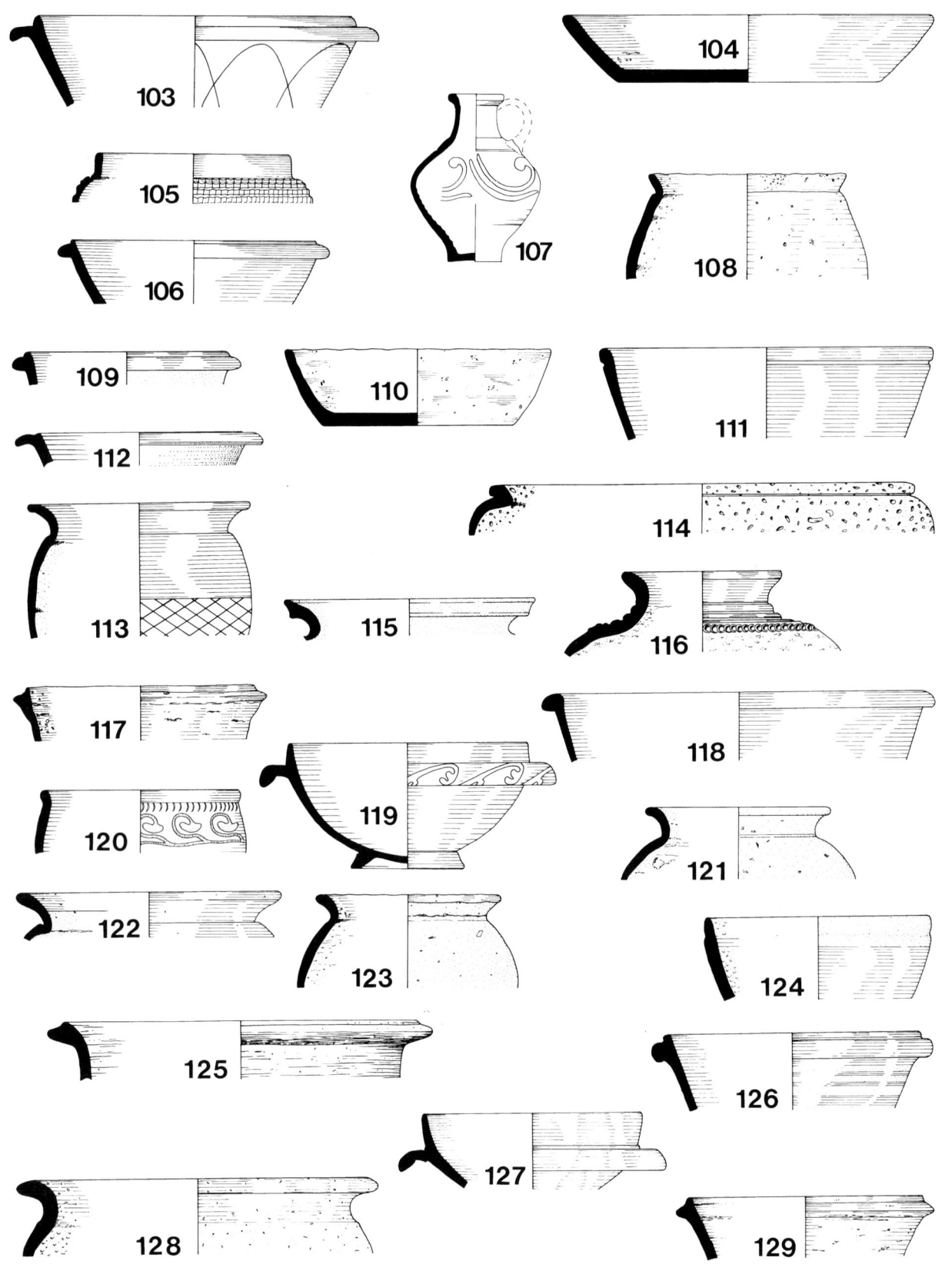

Fig. 24 Coarse pottery (¼).

No. 100   Dish with upright rim of grey sandy ware. Common late-second to early-third century type. (ORPV–89–313)
No. 101   Beaker sherd with applied dolphin design of Nene Valley ware with all-over dark red-brown colour-coat. A.D. 150–200. (ORPV–89–313)

East Corridor
No. 102   Dish with bead rim of light grey sandy ware with dark grey surfaces. Common during the latter half of the second century A.D. F.62. (ORPV–88–186).

Middle Terrace (Period IV)
No. 103   Dish with flange of dark grey sandy ware with black surfaces. A.D. 250–300. (ORPV–89–323 and 322).
No. 104   Dish with upright rim of grey sandy ware. A.D. 200–250. (ORPV–89–327).
No. 105   Bowl with upright rim of orange-buff sandy ware with all-over red-brown colour-coat. A.D. 270–300. (ORPV–89–326).
No. 106   Dish with flanged rim of grey sandy ware with grey-brown surfaces. A.D. 200–250. (ORPV–89–324).

Room 10
No. 107   Flagon of red-brown colour-coated ware. Late-third century. (ORPV–88–149)
No. 108   Beaker with everted rim of orange grit-tempered ware. Not easily paralleled. (ORPV–88–228).

Room 16
No. 109   Dish with flanged rim of light grey Alice Holt type ware. Compare AH/F 5B.6. A.D. 200–250. (ORPV–88–160)

Room 13B
No. 110   Dish with upright rim of dark grey sandy ware with grey to buff-brown surfaces. Compare KES–1 804. A.D. 250–300. (ORPV–88–115)

Room 14D
No. 111   Dish with upright rim of BB2 ware, or copy. Compare KES–1 732. A.D. 180–220. (ORPV–88–97).
No. 112   Dish with flanged rim of dark grey sandy ware with black surfaces and burnished rim-top. Similar to No. 97. Compare KES–1 755. First half of third century A.D. (ORPV–88–185).
No. 113   Jar with cavetto rim of BB2 ware. Burnished from inside rim to below shoulder. A.D. 180–220. (ORPV–88–102).
No. 114   Cooking pot with bead rim of grey 'corky' ware with buff-brown surfaces. Compare KES–1 280 and 476. Similar to No. 74. Common in West Kent during the late-first century A.D. (ORPV–89–301).

Late Terrace
No. 115   Cooking pot with squared rim of grey NKM/TS, or type, ware. Compare MON.3H5. See also KES–1 642 and 693. A.D. 180–230. (ORPV–88–72)
No. 116   Storage jar with outcurved rim, cordons on neck and stabbing on shoulder of Patch Grove ware with buff-brown surfaces. Compare WK 249 and 322 and DV 204. A.D. 150–200. Similar to No. 150. (ORPV–88–124).

Shaft F51
No. 117   Dish with flanged rim of grey sandy ware with dark grey to black surfaces. Compare KES–1 771. Late-third to fourth century A.D. (ORPV–88–129).

Shaft F58
No. 118   Dish with bead rim of grey sandy NKM/TS ware with dark grey to black surfaces. As MON.5C3. A.D. 180–220. (ORPV–88–154)
No. 119   Bowl with down-turned flange of Oxfordshire colour-coat ware imitating Dr. 38 (YG C52). A.D. 350–400+. (ORPV–88–212).
No. 120   Bowl with upright thickened rim of Oxfordshire colour-coat ware. As YG C82.2 dated A.D. 325–400+. (ORPV–88–211).
No. 121   Cooking pot with outcurved rim of grey coarse sandy ware with dark grey to black surfaces. A.D. 150–200. (ORPV–88–147).
No. 122   Cooking pot with cavetto rim of light grey sandy NKM/TS ware. Compare MON.3J9. Late-second to mid/late-third century A.D. (ORPV–88–241).

Fig. 25. Coarse pottery (¼).

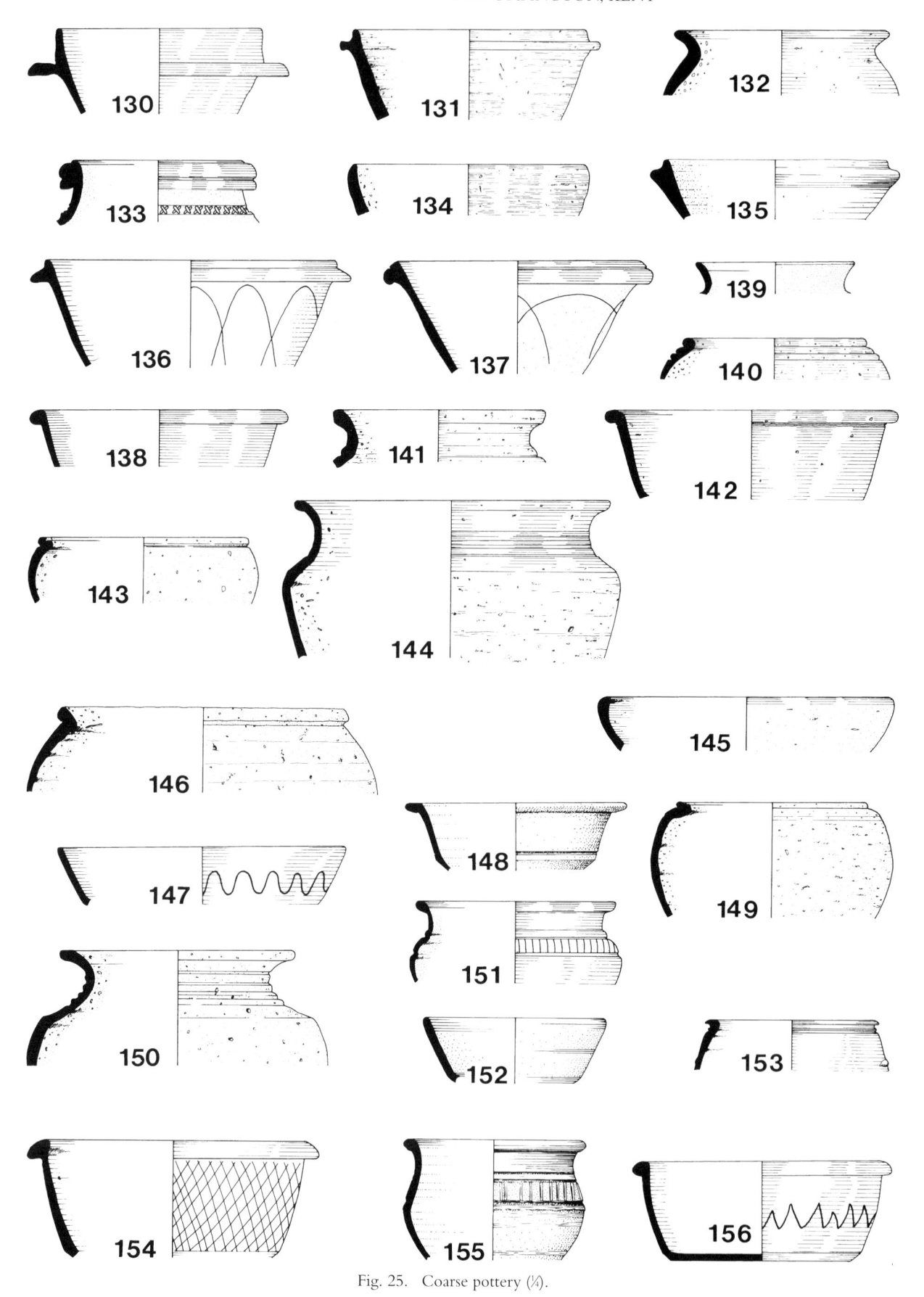

West Ditch F1

No. 123 Cooking pot with outcurved rim of light grey sandy ware with dark grey surfaces. Similar to No. 121. (ORPV–88–10).

No. 124 Dish with upright rim of light grey coarse sandy ware with dark grey exterior and light grey to buff interior surface. Compare WK Nos. 403, 415 and 440 and KES–1 611. Late-third or fourth century A.D. (ORPV–88–10).

No. 125 Dish/bowl with outcurved flanged rim of grey to buff coarse sandy ware with orange-brown exterior and grey to buff-brown interior surface. Compare POL 196 of late-second to early-fourth century A.D. (ORPV–88–14)

No. 126 Dish with beaded rim of light grey sandy ware with grey to buff-brown exterior and grey interior surface. Compare WK 400 and KES–1 809. Late-third to fourth centuries A.D. (ORPV–88–26).

No. 127 Bowl with downturned flange of Oxfordshire ware imitating Dr. 38 (as YG C51), A.D. 240–400+. (ORPV–88–26).

No. 128 Cooking pot with outcurved rim of orange-brown to buff; calcite-gritted ware with buff-brown surfaces and dark grey rim. Probably fourth century A.D. (ORPV–88–28).

No. 129 Dish with flanged rim of grey sandy ware (with some calcite grits) with dark grey to black burnished surfaces. Compare WK 387, DV 196, KES–1 771, 777 and DOV–1 218. Late-third and fourth centuries A.D. (ORPV–88–279).

Soil Deposits over the Villa

No. 130 Bowl with side flange of Oxfordshire colour-coat ware imitating Dr. 38 (YG C51). A.D. 240–400+. (ORPV–88–13).

No. 131 Dish with flange of grey coarse sandy ware with grey-brown surfaces. Common fourth century A.D. type. (ORPV–88–13).

No. 132 Jar with outcurved rim of red-brown 'grog' tempered ware with dark grey to black surfaces. Fourth century A.D. (ORPV–88–257).

No. 133 Storage jar with folded rim of Alice Holt ware. As AH/F 1A, 16 of fourth century A.D. date. (ORPV–88–3).

No. 134 Dish with plain rim of brown sand and 'grog' tempered ware with black to buff-brown surfaces. A.D. 270–350. (ORPV–88–172).

No. 135 Dish with stub-flange of light brown sandy ware with grey-brown surfaces. Compare WK 387, KES–1 777 and DV 196. Fourth century A.D. (ORPV–88–61).

No. 136 Dish with flange of Alice Holt ware. As AH/F 5B, 3. A.D. 220–270. (ORPV–88–61).

No. 137 Dish with thickened flange of Alice Holt ware. As AH/F 5B, 8. A.D. 270–420. (ORPV–88–61).

No. 138 Dish with bead rim of grey sandy NKM/TS ware. As MON.5C1. A.D. 180–220. (ORPV–88–213).

Pit-Line A

No. 139 Beaker with outcurved rim of light grey fine sandy ware with grey-brown surfaces. A.D. 120–170. (F.3). (ORPV–88–17).

No. 140 Cooking pot with bead rim of grey Patch Grove type ware with dark brown surfaces. Compare form with WK 247. Late-first century A.D. (F.29). (ORPV–88–22).

No. 141 Cooking pot with outcurved rim of light grey Patch Grove type ware with dark grey surfaces. Compare WK 249, KES–1 535 and DV 206. Late-first to early-second century A.D. (F.3). (ORPV–88–41).

No. 142 Pie dish with bead rim of grey sandy ware with grey-brown surfaces. Compare DOV–1 508 and 821 and DOV-2 107 and 108. Common during mid-second century A.D. (F.9). (ORPV–88–30).

No. 143 Cooking pot with recessed bead rim of light grey sandy ware with 'grog' and calcite grit inclusions. Grey exterior and light brown interior surface. Compare form to WK 224. A.D. 75–120. (F.9). (ORPV–88–30).

No. 144 Cooking pot with outcurved rim of light grey Patch Grove ware with buff-brown surfaces. Common in West Kent during first to early-second centuries A.D. (F.9). (ORPV–88–36).

No. 145 Dish with plain inturned rim of red-brown sandy ware with red-brown to grey surfaces. Compare DV 222. Late-first to early-second century A.D. (F.14). (ORPV–88–42).

Pit-Line B

No. 146 Cooking pot with everted squared rim of brown coarse gritty ware with dark grey to black surfaces. Romanised copy of native bead rim cooking pot. Late-first century A.D. (F.47). (ORPV–88–99).

No. 147 Dish with upright rim of BB2 ware. Compare DOV-1 880 and DOV-2 100, A.D. 180–200. (F.22). (ORPV–88–208).

No. 148 Bowl with flanged rim of grey sandy Highgate Wood type ware. Second century. (F.22). (ORPV–88–76).

No. 149   Small cooking pot with bead rim of Patch Grove ware with grey-brown surfaces. Common in West Kent during second half of first century A.D. (F.30). (ORPV–88–104).
No. 150   Storage jar with outcurved rim of Patch Grove ware with buff-brown surfaces. Common in West Kent during late-first century to mid-second century A.D. Compare WK 249. (F.31). (ORPV–88–53).
No. 151   Beaker with cordons on shoulder of grey sandy Highgate Wood type ware. Late-first or early-second century A.D. (F.33). (ORPV–88–54).

Pit-Line C

No. 152   Dish with upright rim of dark grey to black sandy ware. A.D. 180–200. (F.41). (ORPV–88–51).
No. 153   Beaker with cornice rim of off-white colour-coat (poss. Colchester) ware with dark grey to red-brown surfaces. Compare DOV-1 391 dated second half of second century A.D. (F.40). (ORPV–88–52).

Miscellaneous Pits

No. 154   Dish with bead rim and lattice pattern of BB2 ware. Compare DOV-1 553 and 794 and DOV-2 100. A.D. 150–200. (F.8). (ORPV–88–29).
No. 155   Jar with outcurved rim of light grey Highgate Wood type ware. Compare WK 178, 240 and 242. Early second century A.D. (F.95). (ORPV–88–156).
No. 156   Dish with bead rim and wavy line decoration of BB2 ware. Compare DOV-1 540 and 573. Other examples occur in DOV-2. A.D. 120–160. (F.95). (ORPV–88–156).
No. 157   Dish with upright rim of dark grey sandy ware with dark grey surfaces. Compare WK Nos. 328 and 428 and DOV-1 Nos. 474 and 478. A.D. 180–220. (F.98). (ORPV–88–286).
No. 158   Cooking pot with bead rim of grey 'corky' ware with buff-brown to dark grey exterior and red-brown interior surface. Compare WK 157, 158 and 160. A.D. 70–100. (F.78). (ORPV–88–248).
No. 159   Complete jar with outcurved rim of handmade grey grog-tempered ware with mottled dark grey and brown surfaces. A.D. 350–450. (F.90). (ORPV–88–275).
No. 160   Jar with out-turned rim of dark red-brown sandy ware with red-brown surfaces. Compare WK 319, 327, 354 and 366 and DOV-2 203 dated to the late-second or early-third century A.D. (F.87). (ORPV–88–259).
No. 161   Flagon with ringed rim and handle of buff to orange fine sandy ware with cream-white slip over exterior surface. Probably mid-second to early-third century A.D. (F.87). (ORPV–88–259).
No. 162   Dish with flanged rim of dark grey sandy ware with 'grog' inclusions. Red-brown to grey-brown surfaces. Compare WK 373, 377 and 387. Fourth century A.D. (F.107). (ORPV–89–343).
No. 163   Jar with outcurved rim of grey coarse sandy ware with some 'grog' inclusions. Grey to grey-brown surfaces. A.D. 270–300. (F.107). (ORPV–89–342).
No. 164   Beaker with everted rim, indented and with slip decoration of off-white colour-coat (Nene Valley or New Forest) ware with dark grey to black metallic surfaces. A.D. 270–300. (F.107). (ORPV–89–342).

Miscellaneous Ditches/Gullies

No. 165   Cooking pot with outcurved rim of dark grey coarse sandy ware. Probably late-second century A.D. (F.54). (ORPV–88–168).
No. 166   Beaker with outcurved rim of light grey sandy ware with dark grey surfaces. Compare WK 341. Late-second century A.D. (F.54). (ORPV–88–168).
No. 167   Beaker with upright rim of grey fine sandy Alice Holt ware silver-grey slip to exterior surface, burnished on inside of rim. Compare DOV-1 461 and 684 there dated A.D. 150–200. (F.54). (ORPV–88–256).
No. 168   Dish with upright rim of dark grey sandy ware with grey surfaces and burnished interior. Compare examples from Darenth (WK and DV) and Dover (DOV-1 and 2) and KES-1, 557. A.D. 180–220. (F.81). (ORPV–88–246).
No. 169   Dish with bead rim of red-brown fine sandy ware with buff surfaces. Compare examples from Darenth (WK and DV) and Dover (DOV-1 and 2). A.D. 180–220. (F.81). (ORPV–88–246).

Miscellaneous Post-Holes

No. 170   Beaker with out-turned rim of light grey-brown sandy ware with grey surfaces. Compare DOV-1 515. Early-second century A.D. (F.16). (ORPV–88–44).
No. 171   Beaker with everted rim of grey sandy NKM/TS ware. Common during late-second century A.D. (F.69). (ORPV–88–110).
No. 172   Dish with bead rim of grey sandy ware with dark grey to black surfaces. A.D. 180–220. (F.42). (ORPV–88–112).

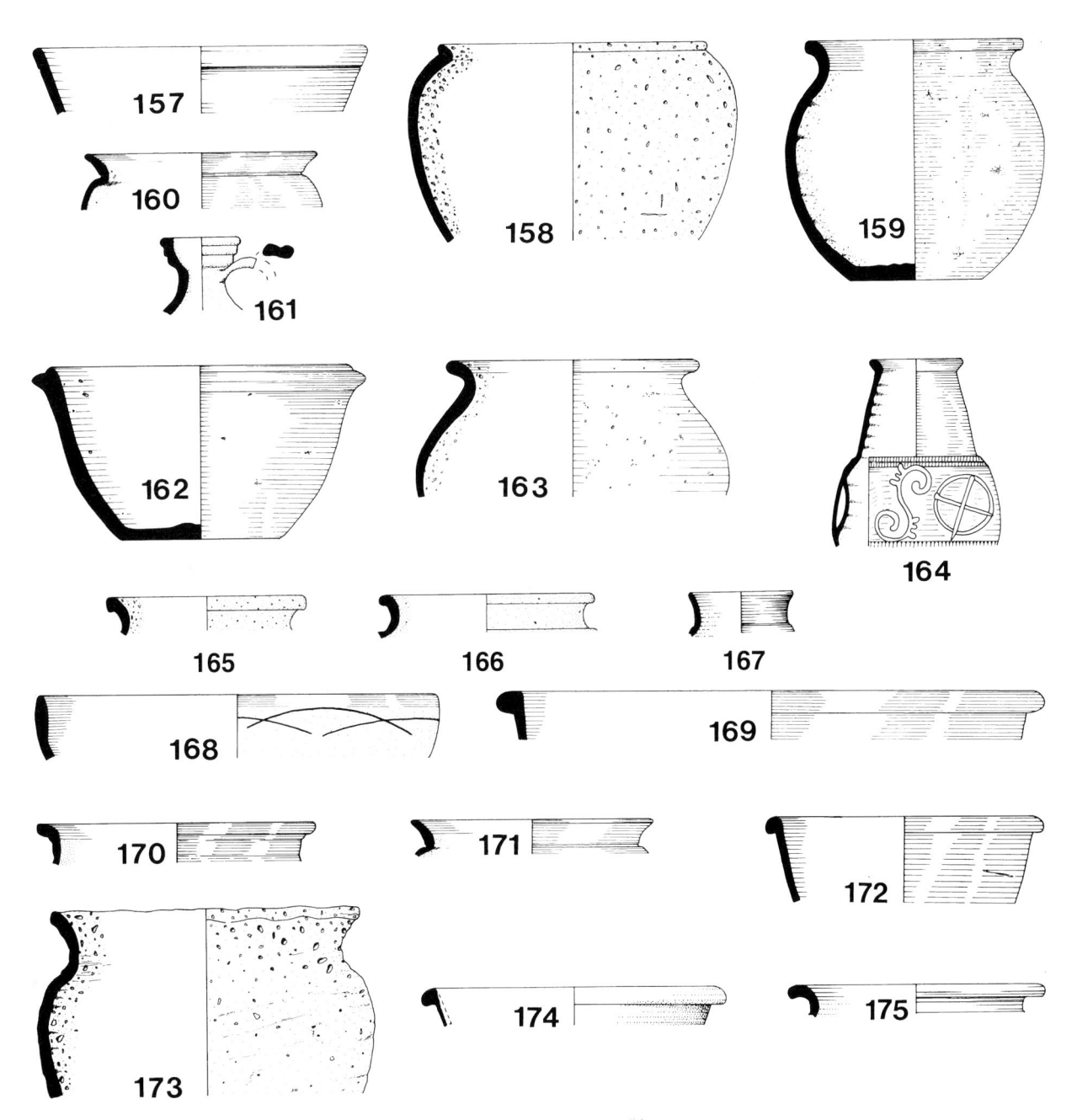

Fig. 26. Coarse pottery (¼).

Post-Roman Hearth

No. 173 Cooking pot with out-turned rim of buff to red-brown shell-tempered ware. 11–12th century A.D. (ORPV–88–65).

No. 174 Dish with bead rim of buff sandy NKM/TS ware. Compare MON.4A2. Probably A.D. 150–200. (ORPV–88–66).

No. 175 Beaker with outcurved rim of buff sandy NKM/TS ware. As MON.5C1. A.D. 120–250. (ORPV–88–66).

Abbreviations in the Text
AH/F = Alice Holt/Farnham 1979 (Ref. 39)
DOV-1 = Dover 1981 (Ref. 40)
DOV-2 = Dover 1989 (Ref. 41)
DV = Darent Valley 1984 (Ref. 42)
KES-1 = Keston 1991 (Ref. 43)
MON = Monaghan 1987 (Ref. 44)
NKM/TS = North Kent Marsh/Thameside (Ref. 45)
POL = Pollard 1988 (Ref. 46)
WK = West Kent 1973 (Ref. 47)
YG = Young 1977 (Ref. 48)

G. THE PAINTED PLASTER (NOS. 176–189)

A total of 956 fragments of Roman wall plaster was found on the villa site during the 1988–89 excavations. This included two small *in situ* areas close to floor-levels (probably dados) and a large section of plaster which had collapsed onto the floor of the West Corridor. This was largely articulated, though facedown, but it was possible to lift this carefully to provide the only substantial detailed evidence for a decorative scheme inside the villa (see below). All the fragments have been subjected to a fabric-analysis, by Peter Keller, who has identified seven fabrics (Fabrics A–G), of which five account for the great majority. Details are held in the archive.

The area which these fragments cover when now laid out is barely 8 sq. m. The wide range of colours, fabrics and locations on the site show that painted plaster was very probably used in every room and certainly in the West Corridor. The original surface-area covered could well have been in excess of 500 sq. m. and thus a very small percentage has survived on the site. Whilst this may seem remarkable it roughly corresponds to the amount of superstructure also missing.

The 800 fragments not *in situ* or fallen, were found both inside and behind the villa, mainly in six large groups. Comparatively little came from the villa rooms which had mostly been cleared by earlier work. The Early Terrace, filled with soil and large amounts of domestic rubbish of Antonine date, contained only ten small fragments of plain red and white, but including red and blue joining bands and a floral design (Nos. 177–8). These must have come from the Period I or II rooms.

Another 15 fragments came from the occupation soils in Room 15 (built in Period II and demolished in Period IV). These were all plain white, blue or red and painted onto a thick layer of *opus signinum* (Fabric C). Two white pieces were slightly convex and may represent mouldings. The dump over Room 15 (probably thrown down during the Period IV work), contained another 65 fragments, again mostly plain red, white, green, yellow, but with some red splashes on a white ground, perhaps a dado. All this could only have come from the Period I to Period III rooms.

The Middle Terrace (Period IV) was also filled with soil and this produced another 43 fragments of plaster. This included plain red, white and green on yellow, but also the corner of a blue frame lined internally with maroon and enclosing a white field.

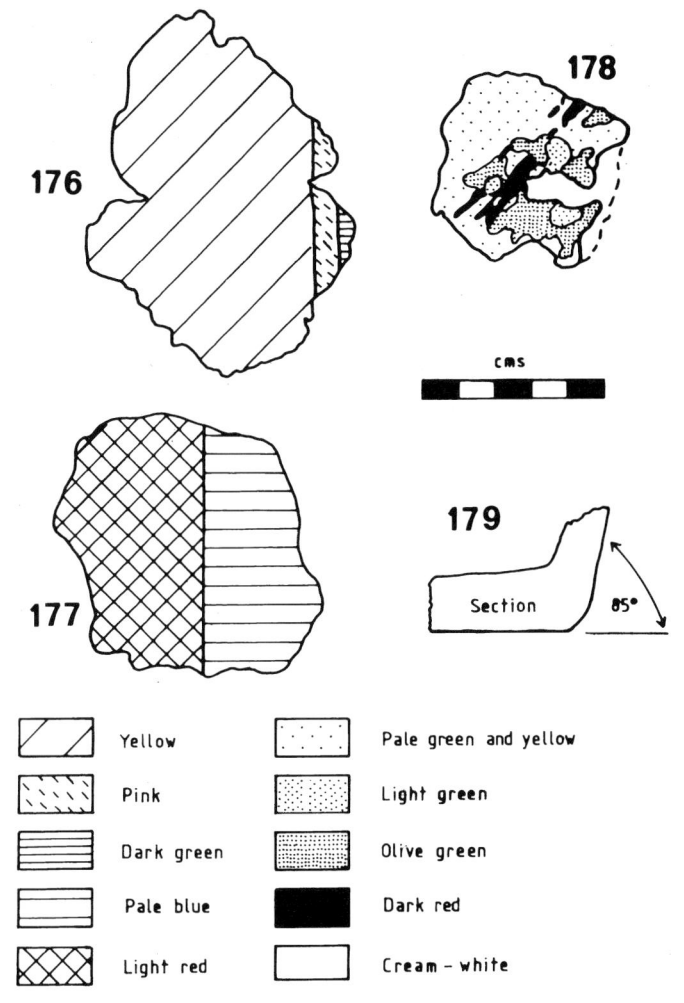

Fig. 27. Painted wall plaster, designs on Fabric A

The fill of the Late Terrace (Period V) produced 43 more fragments, mainly plain white, pink, red and green. One showed a decorative curving line in brown inside a thin frame, two narrow stripes over red on white and other fragments with red dots on a white ground, possibly the dado. A small piece showing red and green could represent a floral design.

Only ten fragments of plaster came from the rubble in Room 10 (Period V) and this was mostly red and white (No. 184). It included a fragment with two red stripes on a pink field and a blue band, lined with a maroon stripe by a white field (No. 181). Some 74 fragments came from the rubble filling of the robbed hypocaust in Room 13B (Period V) and this was mainly badly weathered. Whilst some red and yellow (Nos. 176 and 186) were present the predominant colour was plain green (No. 185). Another 39 fragments were also found in the damaged hypocaust channels in Room 14D (Period V) and these included white, green and some red, the latter including bands, suggesting broad panels.

Another large group of plaster, including the largest and most decorative fragments, came from the soils dumped in the abandoned north end of the West Corridor, containing late-

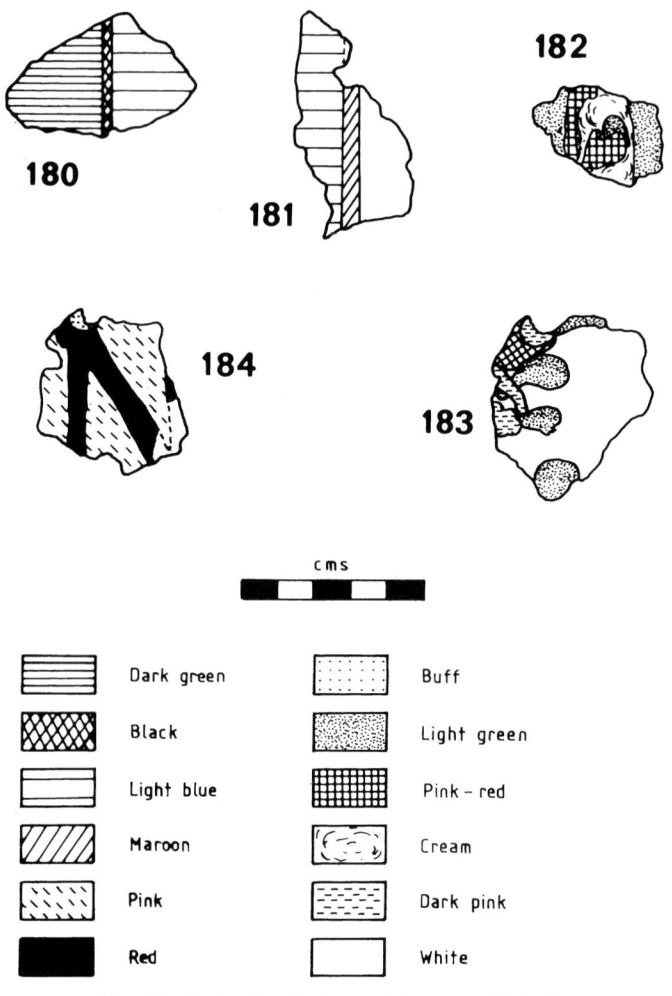

Fig. 28. Painted wall plaster, designs on Fabric B

third century pottery (Period V). This included part of a capital adjacent to a yellow panel with a wide orange/pink border above (No. 187); part of a yellow panel with a red border (No. 188) and a green plant design on a yellow panel (No. 189). These three were the same fabrics and formed part of the same design, somewhat similar to the designs in the Painted House at Dover. Other fragments were yellow, red or pink and there was part of a red respond.

A pit (F.107) cut through the floor and south-west hypocaust channel in Room 14D (Period V) contained a substantial 254 fragments of plaster. All seem to have been burnt *in situ*, whilst the original colours seem to have been plain cream, grey, orange and some with a maroon floral pattern.

Finally, the soils over the villa produced another 62 fragments, including plain white, red, some blue-green and one piece with cream stripes on pink and green and a floral design (Nos. 179, 180 and 182, 183).

As regards the *in situ* and fallen plaster, the dado on the cross-wall in the West Corridor was mostly white, but showed two vertical bands of red each at least 6 cm. wide and a maximum of 42 cm. apart. The dado in Room 14C was pink/white flecked with red splashes.

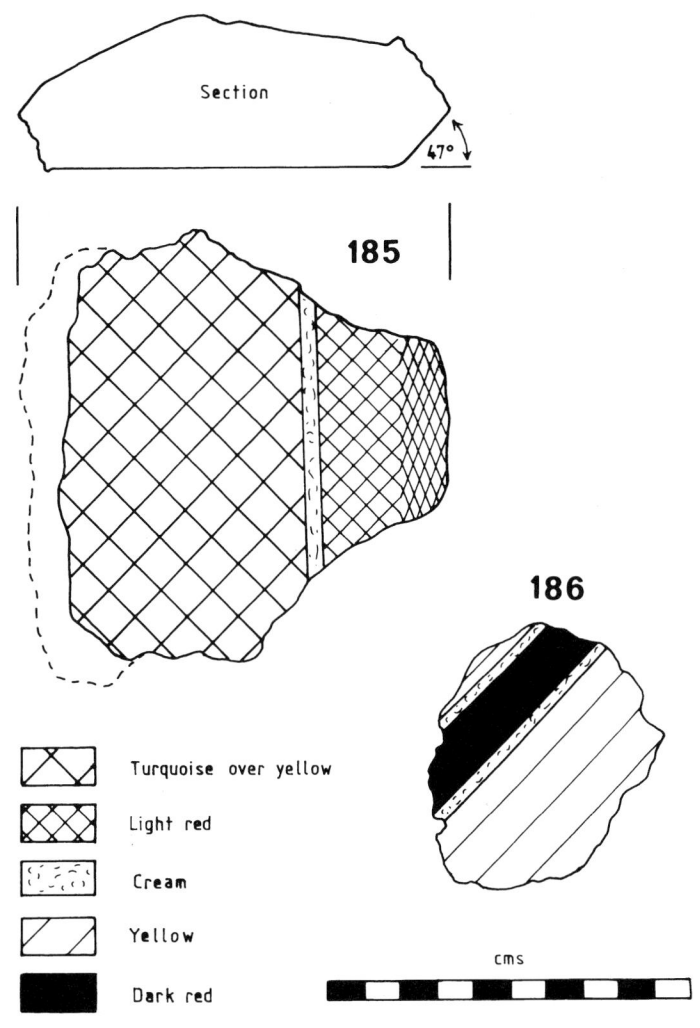

Fig. 29. Painted wall plaster, designs on Fabric F

The fallen panel (Fig. 31) came from the junction of the external corridor wall and the inserted cross-wall, just outside Room 7. The cross-wall was only 75 cm. wide to the certain door-opening here and seems too narrow for the fallen plaster. On balance the plaster (Fabric A) probably slewed off the inside face of the outside wall of the West Corridor. The design (Fig. 32) consists of a horizontal band of red (45 mm. min.), perhaps placed above a dado consisting of vertical red bands and white panels as found *in situ* nearby. Another vertical red band (26 mm. wide), then separated two large rectangular white panels outlined with a green stripe (11 mm.). The stripes are some 48 mm. and 56 mm., respectively, from the dividing red vertical. The left-hand panel seems to be at least 250 mm. wide and the right-hand panel is complete at about 420 mm. The height of the panel seems to have been about 1.020 m.

The vertical red band joins a broader red horizontal band (53 mm.) at a total height of about 1.215 m. which is surmounted by a narrow horizontal white panel (perhaps 120 mm.), again bordered in red (20 mm.) enclosing another green stripe (9 mm.). Allowing for a bottom dado of about 600 mm. the overall height represented here is about 2.050 m. A normal frieze above this might have increased the overall height to about 2.40 m. The panels

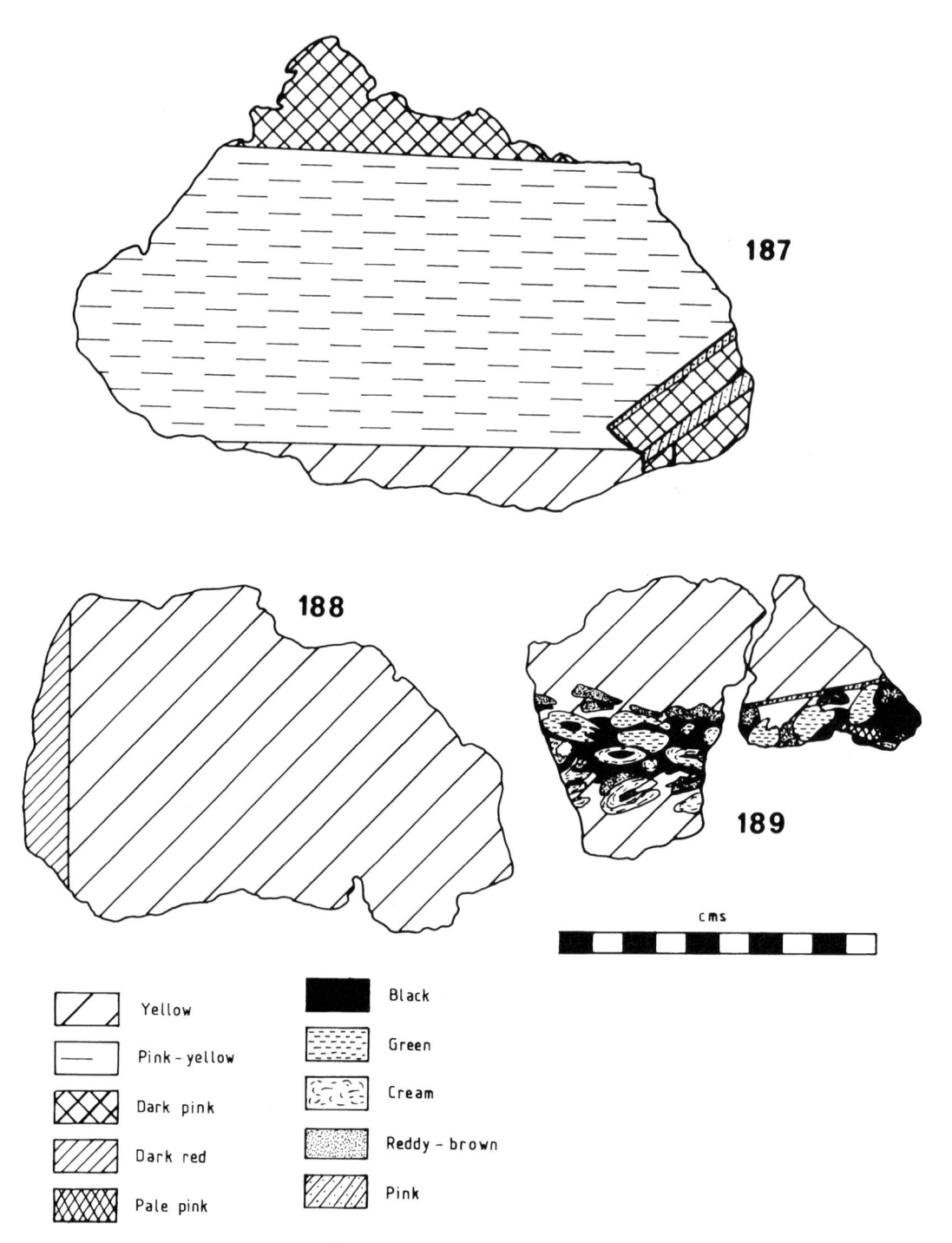

Fig. 30. Painted wall plaster, designs on Fabric D

THE EXCAVATED OBJECTS 85

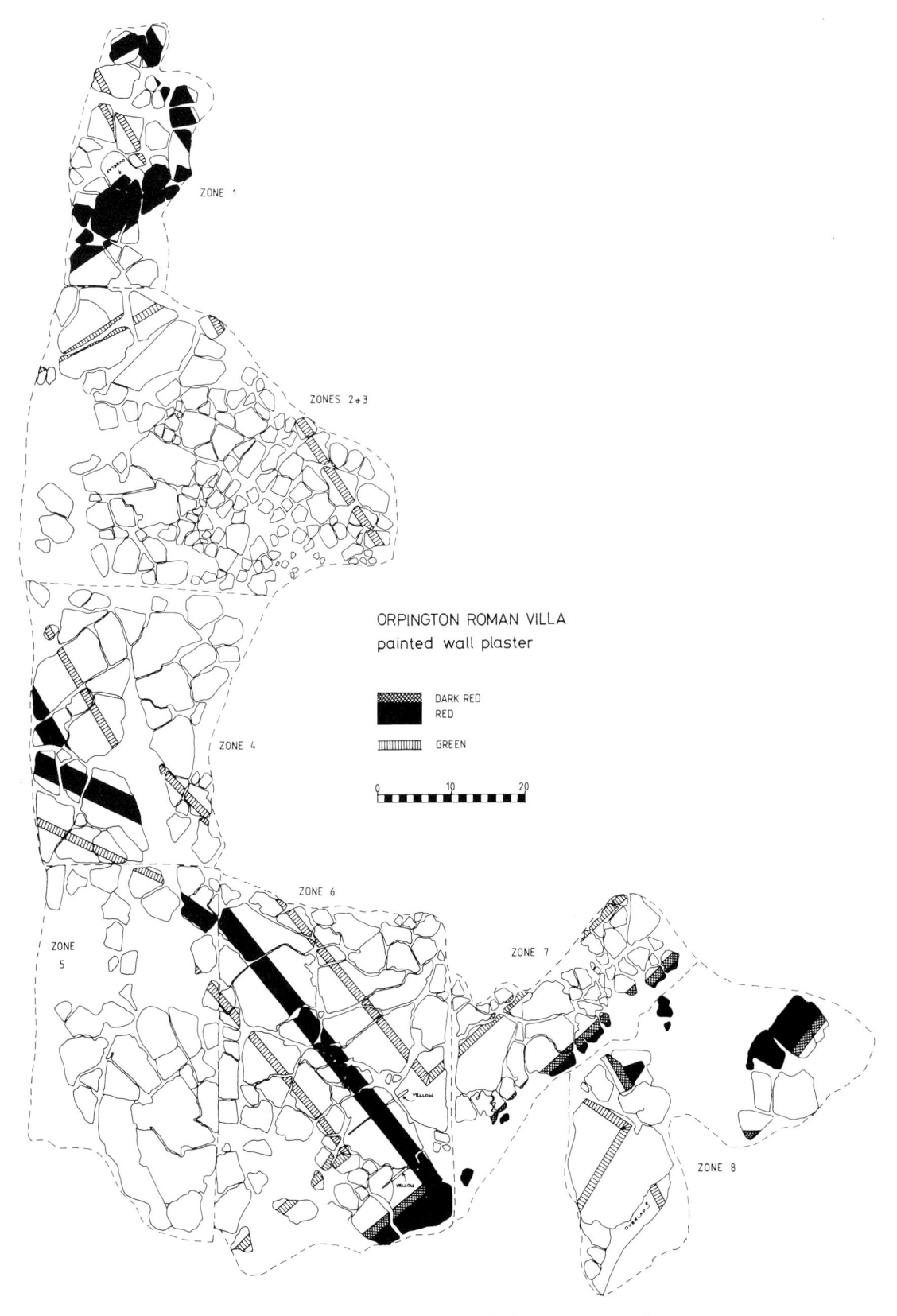

Fig. 31. Area of fallen painted wall plaster, West Corridor

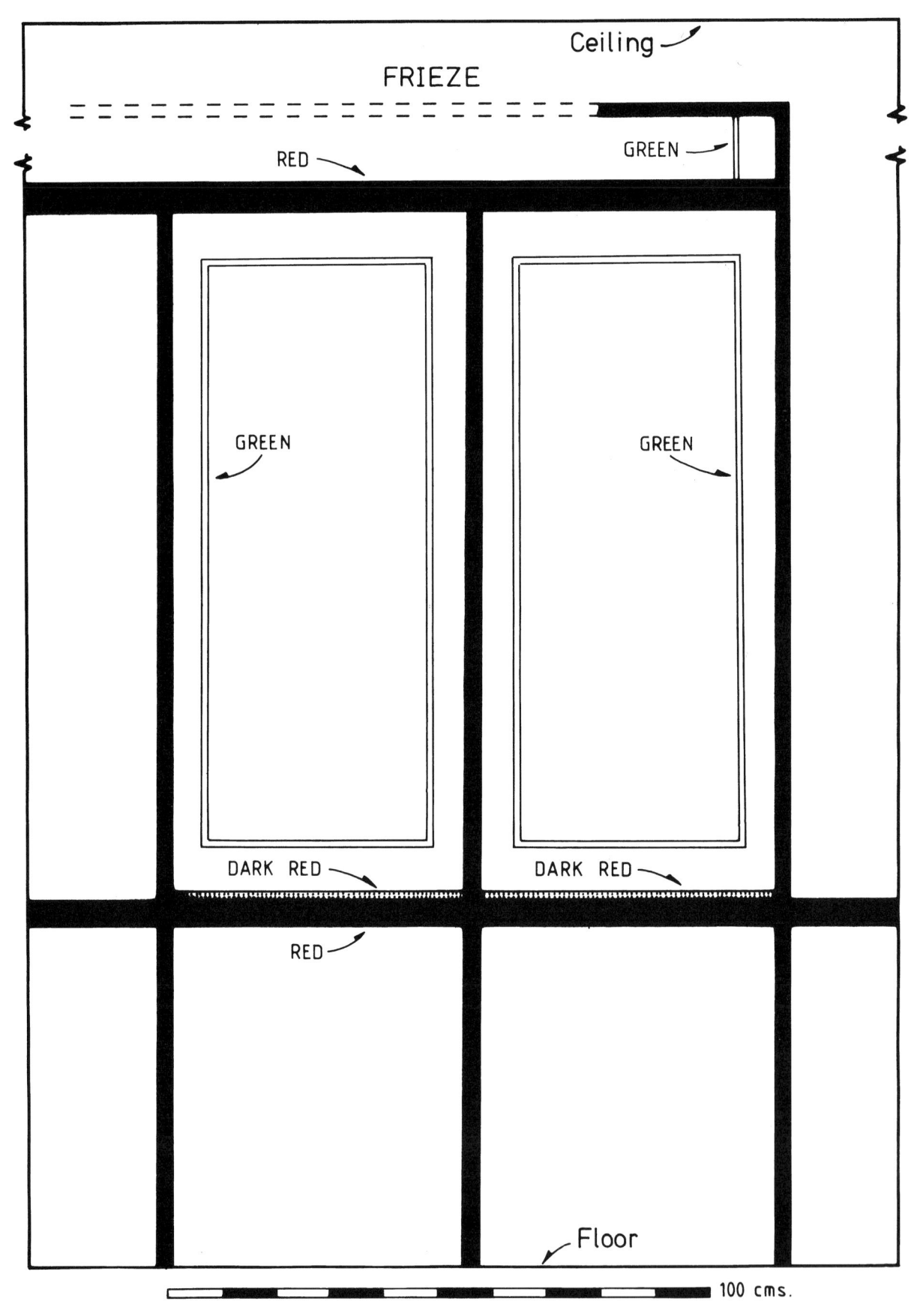

Fig. 32. Reconstructed painted design, West Corridor

are not decorated and the overall ground is white. This rather typical and plain rectilinear pattern was used here in a domestic corridor.

Although very little can be said with certainty about the decoration of the main rooms the fragments from the site give some clues. Although much of the plaster is plain and in a range of colours, there were clearly some rectilinear panels in various colours. There were also some highly decorative elements including floral and architectural arrangements. It is impossible to know how extensive these were, but both the latter are similar to elements in the Roman Painted House at Dover (Ref. 49) and could reflect extensive schemes, probably in the main rooms.

In addition to the plaster found in 1988–89 there are three more boxes of plaster listed from the site in earlier years. Some 170 fragments were handed to Bromley Museum some years ago, but some have no associated label and must be regarded with care. Much of it has an 'O' designation and clearly came from the 1955–61 excavations and its fabric and colours match some of those from the more recent work. In total it adds no additional detail. Another 19 fragments of plaster in two small boxes (marked Fordyce) are said to be from the villa site, but their fabrics do not seem to match those from the complete excavation. It seems best to consider these as from another site.

H. THE OTHER OBJECTS

Comparatively few small-finds were recovered during the excavation and the majority of them are illustrated and described (Nos. 1–38). To these can be added a fragment of a quern, of millstone grit, found in the fill of the West Ditch dug in the 4th century, but containing some earlier material. A fragment of white marble was recovered from Shaft F.58, but there is a risk here of intrusion. Fragments of bone needles and pins were found and also a bone with two holes drilled in it. There were also several corroded objects of iron, bronze and lead.

A total of 164 fragments of Roman glass (Nos. 31–38) was recovered during the excavations in 1988–9 from about 60 identified deposits/contexts. The majority consists of small fragments, but about a dozen pieces are 5 cm. long, or longer. The largest fragment is 12 cm. long.

A provisional study suggests that 71 pieces came from small windows and the other 93 from a variety of vessels. All the window fragments are either green, pale green or just occasionally green-white. To a greater, or lesser, extent all is translucent. Much of this window glass has either a matt finish on one side, a matt finish on both sides or is polished on one of both sides. Five of the fragments have bevelled edges.

The vessel glass is mostly green, but includes some that is white, blue and amber. Square bottles, bowls and necked vessels are represented. Only about seven are decorated, either with ribs, trails or even letters.

The largest group came from the dumped soils filling the Early Terrace, directly associated with pottery dating to the second half of the second century and no later than about A.D. 220. Here some 32 window fragments and 25 vessel fragments produced a total of 57 pieces. At least two large bottles are represented.

Of some 352 individual soil deposit/contexts registered during the excavation, about 65 contained a total of 170 struck flints and 153 fire-cracked stones. All of these probably relate to pre-Roman activity on the site and appear to represent a late-Neolithic or Early Bronze Age land-use. The great majority of the flints came from Roman soil deposits, directly associated with pottery of 2nd–4th centuries, but very few were recovered from the pre-villa soils and only four from the Early Ditch. Eight flakes came from the undated Gully (F.21) on the west side of the villa, which was clearly dug early in the history of the site.

Most of the flints are either grey, grey-brown or brown-black and a few are black. These are largely struck flakes or waste, but two probable blades and four scrapers, with secondary working, can be identified. One possible arrow-head, perhaps an unfinished tanged type, may be present, whilst a large hammer-stone was recovered from a disturbed deposit. No cores seem to be included.

Collectively, this is a small collection and represents only a slight scatter across the area excavated. Such a scatter could have covered several acres, or even much of the hillside. Another 20 struck flints had been found on the site in 1955–61.

I. BUILDING MATERIALS

Whilst no detailed attempt has been made here, or indeed often elsewhere, to study the total building materials used on the site, some basic quantities can be calculated.

THE WALLS

The principal building element used at Crofton was flint, obtained locally and indirectly from the Upper Chalk. Simple measurements suggest that each linear metre of flint coursing contained eight flints, which increased to about 30 flints through the thickness of the wall. There seems to have been about ten courses in each vertical metre of wall so that one linear square-metre of complete wall might contain about 300 flints.

The walls under the most extensive layout (Period III) seem to have a combined length of about 230 m. and the average height was probably 3.00 m. These figures thus suggest that a total of about 200,000 flints were required at Crofton during the Roman period. Some allowances must be made for any wall thickness reduction, door and window-openings, a possible open verandah on the east side, but also extensive flint foundations in Periods II–IV. Even then, it seems likely that at least 180,000 flints would have been needed. This number might be substantially reduced if part of the building had been provided with a wooden-frame.

All these flints had to be collected from the local area, transported in carts and then individually handled by the wall builders. It seems likely that the total weight was probably in excess of 400 tons during the life of the Roman site.

THE ROOF (PLATE XXVIII)

It seems clear from the large numbers of broken roof tiles found along most of the west side of the villa, that it was roofed entirely with large tiles. These were both tegulae and imbrices, familiar on so many Roman sites in Britain and on the Continent. During the most extensive Period III, the roof probably covered about 600 sq. m, allowing for a low pitch and modest eaves. If the tegulae tiles built into the west wall of Room 6 were typical (at about 45 × 30 cm.) then it is possible to roughly calculate the total number. Allowing for the required overlap it seems that at least 5,000 tegulae would be needed to cover the whole villa and perhaps the same number of imbreces. Any ancilliary buildings may have needed many more.

THE TESSELLATED FLOORS

It seems clear that Rooms 1, 2, 4, 5 and 11 and also the East Corridor were all tessellated with large, plain red tesserae. It seems likely that Room 3 was too! The surviving area of tessellation in Room 11 shows that there were about 1,000 tesserae in a square-metre. There is no reason to suppose that the rooms and corridors were not fully tessellated and simple calculations show that each room might thus require about 25,000 tesserae. Allowing for all the rooms and corridor it seems possible that some 240 sq. m. might have been surfaced in this way and that about 250,000 tesserae would have been required. Even if these were not fully covered in this way it is clear that very large numbers of tesserae were used. It seems unlikely that all these could have been made from existing tiles on the site and the probability is that a large stock was imported onto the site.

Of special interest were four small tesserae, three white and one grey. The latter and a white were found in the Early Terrace, one white in Pit F15 and one white unstratified. These suggest the presence of at least one small mosaic panel, perhaps in a major room, relating to either Periods I–III. Significantly, two more white tesserae were found in 1955–61 and help support this suggestion. It is, however, possible that these tesserae were introduced casually onto the site in Roman times.

THE WALL, PILAE AND FLUE TILES

Large numbers of broken tiles were found on the site, mostly in the roof fall along the west wall of the villa. Many others came from disturbed deposits, but the cost of carrying out a definitive study would be prohibitive. The better examples have been placed in store and many others buried on the site.

The only complete wall tiles are about 20 used as capstones in the hypocaust in Room 14D (Period V), which were mostly 43 × 30 × 3 cm. Another eight were found built into the walls of Room 10 (also Period V) which are largely the same size.

The pilae tiles were only found in Rooms 10 and 16 and of the 11 which survived these were mostly 21 × 21 × 3 cm. About 170 would have been needed in Room 16 and about 420 in Room 10, perhaps a batch of 600 in all. These were standard size tiles and were probably brought onto the site by the builders. Although no complete bridging tile was found it seems that Rooms 10 and 16 would together have needed about 65 of these very large standard tiles and these too must have been brought to the site.

Only fragments of box-flue tiles were found on the site, with only three remaining *in situ*. These were probably about 42 cm. in length, about 16 × 10 cm. in width and had a pair of opposite lateral holes at the centre of the long sides. These were roughly circular in shape and helped key the flue-tiles into the walls. Most flue-tiles showed external combing for similar keying and one had a roughly diamond-shaped pattern applied with a roller die.

It seems clear that Room 6 would have had six vertical wall-flues, Room 10 about eight, Room 16 four and the large Rooms 13B and 14D perhaps four-eight each. In all some 26–34 vertical flues were probably provided. With each box-flue tile about 42 cm. in length, each vertical flue probably required about eight box-flue tiles to reach roof or eaves level. If so, about 200–270 would have been needed and these very special tiles would certainly have to be brought to the site.

Six fragments of box-flue tile appear to have been parts of rectangular voussoirs. The smaller (lower) face seems to have been about 15 × 15 cm. and the larger (vertical) face appear to have been 19 cm. long, tapering down by about 1 cm. All are combed and three have a crude 3 cm. hole punched through the centre of the larger side. These may never have been included in a vaulted roof.

CHAPTER IV

DISCUSSION

A. THE SITE

Whatever the early origins of the site it is quite clear that the main Roman villa-house was conscientiously built well-up the steep slope of the west side of the Cray Valley. The building followed the natural contours and lay about 20 m. below the crest of the hill and about 30 m. above the adjacent bottom of the valley. This contrasts with the great majority of corresponding buildings in the Cray, Darent or Medway valleys of West Kent which were built in the valley bottoms, on or close to the actual rivers. It seems clear that the latter were important for transporting produce and providing abundant water.

The obvious parallel for such an elevated position lies at Keston (Ref. 1), only some 5 km. to the south-west, where the Roman villa complex was also placed across the shoulder of the hill. The Keston site flanked a largely dry valley, but there were abundant springs above the site and water was piped from there to the various buildings. It must be that springs existed close to the Crofton site and although not now apparent, 19th century maps show small streams then running west of the villa.

B. PREHISTORIC EVIDENCE

The earliest evidence of settlement on the site is represented by about 153 fire-cracked stones, about 190 struck flint flakes and a single potsherd, all clearly of prehistoric type and probably reflecting a modest use of part of the broader hillside in Neolithic, or perhaps Early Bronze Age times. A dense concentration of fire-cracked stones (F.13), three adjacent pits (F.5–7) and a shallow gully (F.31), could just represent a small settlement-site, but more evidence is needed.

C. THE ROMAN FARMSTEAD

It is clear that the site was first substantially occupied in the 1st century A.D., probably by a modest farmstead. The so-called Belgic hut beneath the villa, identified by earlier work can now be seen as an early ditch, whilst the pottery from the site suggests that it was established at about the middle of the 1st century A.D. Although no structure dating from the 1st century has been found in the area excavated three early features, two gullies (F.102 and F.104) and a larger ditch (the Early Ditch F.101), seem to have related to such a farmstead. The few objects recovered from them are no later than A.D. 130. The general finds from the site also include about ten samian vessels and perhaps twenty coarse pottery vessels from the second half of the 1st century A.D. These include a samian Form 27 (A.D. 55–70), a Form 30 (A.D. 50–65) and a Form 37 (A.D. 70–85). In addition a mid-1st century brooch, of Hod Hill type, was also found.

The Early Ditch could have formed part of a rectangular enclosure similar to those on other early-Roman sites and may have enclosed a posted-structure, perhaps similar to the early ones at nearby Keston (Period V). Very little archaeological evidence is known from uphill of the villa, where much of the area has been reduced at different times. This tends to favour the area east of the villa for any 1st century structure, but most of that area has been severely damaged by various developments. About 200 m. east of the villa is Station Approach, a site excavated by the Kent Unit ahead of development in 1993. This produced part of an early-Roman enclosure, other ditches and pits, mainly of late-1st and 2nd century date. These either represent a separate site or part of the Crofton site, in which case a much more extensive farmstead is indicated (Ref. 50).

D. THE ROMAN VILLA (FIG. 16)

The first villa-house was a compact rectangular structure, consisting of a range of five rooms (Rooms 1–5) and a West Corridor, some 30 × 10.40 m. and covering an area of about 310 sq. m. The four main rooms were each probably about 5.80 × 5.50 m. and the West Corridor was about 28 m. long and 2.40 m. wide. All the foundations were of rammed chalk and were cut through pre-villa soils and through earlier features, all containing material no later than A.D. 130. An Early Terrace, dug to give access to the back of the Period I house, was filled with a very large amount of Antonine pottery (A.D. 140–180) discarded as domestic rubbish. There can be little doubt that this came from the original house which was probably constructed about A.D. 140–170. The original walls were of mortared flint, though very little of these survived. The chalk and flint could not have been obtained from the actual site, but outcrops occur less than 2 km. to the south. The original floors seem to have been of trodden soil, but it is not known if the original building had glazed windows and plastered walls.

It is difficult to determine the function of each of the six structural elements. The corridor was clearly at the back and could have served for the storage of farm tools, firewood, hardy vegetables and fruit, as well as providing access to the rooms. The central room (Room 3) could be regarded as a principal room, perhaps for dining, with the other four being used either as bedrooms, a kitchen or for storage. Any such storeroom might have been placed at the cooler north end (Room 1), perhaps with an adjacent kitchen (Room 2), with possible bedrooms (Rooms 4 and 5) at the warmer south end of the building.

Probably about A.D. 170–200 (Period II) the uphill, west wall of the West Corridor became unstable and had to be replaced by a new wall built about 40 cm. outside the line of the Period I external wall. This increased the corridor internal width to about 3 m. A new integral cross-wall in the West Corridor created a small north room (Room 7) which contained a door opening into the corridor. The external wall of Room 7 had contained a splayed window opening with its sill about 1.20 m. above the floor. This survived in an extensive section of fallen flint mortared wall and could suggest that the external west wall was of masonry to the full height (perhaps 3 m.) and contained a series of splayed window openings along its length. The widened corridor was provided with an extensive *opus signinum* floor at its southern end and a clay floor at its northern end which extended into Room 7.

A large extra room (Room 15) was built at the south-west corner of the Period I house. This measured about 9.50 × 5.00 m. and with the widened corridor increased the overall area of the villa to about 370 sq. m. The new room was also provided with a thin *opus signinum* floor and may have connected with the West Corridor by means of a common doorway on its north side. An occupation soil in this room was sealed by a later clay floor, in turn covered by more occupation soils. This may have served as a semi-detached kitchen. Sometime during Period II, or just possibly during Period III, a fence-line (Pit-line B) was constructed about 1.00 m. beyond the lip of the Early Terrace. Then, or slightly later, another fence-line (Pit-line C) was built along the lip of the terrace itself. Both seem to have protected the house on its uphill side.

About A.D. 200–225 (Period IIIA) a major building programme extended the villa on the south and east sides. A new block of three rooms (Rooms 12, 13A and 14A) and a passageway (Room 11), were inserted in the angle formed by Room 15 and the south end of the villa. A new East Corridor connected with the new south block and extended along most, or the whole, of the east side of the villa. These additions increased the house to about 37.50 × 14.40 m. which, with the projecting section of Room 15, increased the area to about 560 sq. m., almost double the size of the Period I house. The three new rooms were of varying sizes and that described as Room 13A could have been a narrow passageway providing access from outside. The new East Corridor was 2.90 m. wide and thus matched the enlarged (Period II) West Corridor. The new walls were substantially built and both the East Corridor and the passageway were tessellated with coarse red tesserae.

Inside the original house, Room 5 was divided unequally into two rooms (to create Room 6) and two new cross-walls were inserted in the West Corridor, cutting the Period II floor and creating at least two more rooms (Rooms 8 and 9). The narrow width of Room 8 could suggest that this was intended as an entrance passageway from outside, perhaps leading into Room 4 and certainly into the adjacent corridor. The new passageway (Room 11) and the reduced Room 5 were then tessellated with plain red tesserae and it is likely that the tessellated floors surviving in Rooms 1, 2 and 4 were laid at the same time. No trace of floors survived in the largely missing East Corridor and Room 3, but again it seems likely that these rooms were also tessellated during Period III.

Finally, a small bath or tank (Room 14B) with an *opus signinum* wall-lining was later (Period IIIB) inserted in the south block over part of what had been Room 14A.

These major additions to the original house seem to indicate the increased affluence of the family who were adding refinements, changing some room functions and increasing the number of rooms. Some of this could have been to provide additional accommodation, perhaps indicating an extended family.

Perhaps about A.D. 225–250 (Period IV) minor rebuilding work was undertaken at the south-west corner of the villa. Here Room 15 was demolished and replaced by a broader wall following the original line of the west external wall. Room 15, anyway a modest extension relating to Period II, contrasted clearly with the scale of Periods I and III and was perhaps more expendable. The new room which replaced it (Room 14C), also seems to have removed the earlier bath/tank (Room 14B), was about 5.50 × 5.00 m. and had plastered walls with a dado of pink-white flecked with red.

Sometime between about A.D. 270–300 (Period V) the most drastic programme of alterations was carried out and this changed the whole character of the building. The northern half of the building (Rooms 1–3 and 7–8) was abandoned and a substantial suite of five heated rooms (Rooms 6, 10, 13B, 14D and 16) built in the surviving southern half. This reduced the area of the house to about 20 × 14 m. to make it about 280 sq. m. and thus smaller than the original Period I villa. Clearly, the house had become too large for the occupants and as much of it was 150 years old most of the original part of the building was abandoned and the newer parts converted and fully heated.

The heating systems required the removal of some earlier floors and walls so that deep underfloor hypocausts could be constructed. In Rooms 10 and 16 cleverly constructed pillared hypocausts linked with a channelled hypocaust in Room 6, all being fed from a stoke-hole in Room 9. Rooms 13B and 14D were provided with substantial channelled hypocausts built of tile, chalk and clay and seem to have been fed from a common stoke-hole (not found) on the south side. Both the latter were large rooms, with Room 13B probably being about 8 × 5.50 m. and thus the largest room in the villa. Its position at the paramount south-east corner of the villa may explain its importance for here it overlooked the valley on both the south and east sides. It seems likely that Rooms 4, 5, 11 (passage) and part of the East Corridor remained in use during Period V to create a compact block.

It seems likely that some of the abandoned northern end of the building was demolished to provide materials for the Period V work. A large area of wall-plaster soon fell off the West Corridor Wall and landed on its exposed clay floor where it was promptly buried under Period V rubbish no later than A.D. 300. Two nearby sections of masonry fell westwards, the outer wall falling out on top of fallen roof tiles (from Room 7) and itself soon being covered by soil and rubbish.

Sometime in the fourth century a wide West Ditch was dug behind the villa to take stormwater away from the house in a northerly direction. This was recut once and eventually filled with silt containing fourth century pottery and coins. During the later fourth century when the abandoned walls had largely gone, or in two places collapsed, two shafts and one pit were dug, the former perhaps as abortive wells. One deep shaft (F.51) actually cut through part of the buried foundations and floor of Room 8 and another shaft (F.58) cut through the roof-fall and collapsed wall at the north end outside Room 7. These contained pottery and coins of late-fourth century date. A third pit (F.62) seems to have cut the line of the outer wall of the East Corridor. These pits, fallen walls and plaster and dumped rubbish all help prove that the northern end of the building had largely gone by the fourth century. Three late-Roman coins (of Theodosius and Arcadius) suggest that the site (unlike nearby Keston) was still being used at about A.D. 400, or even a little later.

The major reduction of the structure during the Period V rebuilding work (A.D. 270–300) is of considerable significance in itself. It probably reflects important social and economic changes on the site. It does not, however, appear to be an isolated event. The excavation of the great aisled Roman building at Darenth in 1969 (Ref. 3) showed that it too had undergone a similar reduction during its final Period V (4th century). Indeed, whereas Crofton was reduced from 562 sq. m. to only 280 sq. m. (about 50%), the Darenth aisled building was reduced from 848 sq. m. to about 358 sq. m. (about 42%). The similarity of both the degree of reduction and the method during both final periods is at once apparent. Even the great granary at Horton Kirby, excavated in 1972–73 (Ref. 4) had been reduced in its final phase, but in a rather different way. There was no obvious sign of such major reduction at nearby Keston, though even there the large aisled barn was not rebuilt after burning down in the 3rd century, but little detail of the villa-house had survived. It will be interesting to see if other West Kent villa sites produce similar evidence in the future.

Some extra details are provided by the finds from the site. The 900 fragments of wall-plaster show seven different fabric-types and a range of colours and designs, suggesting painted walls during several periods. Whilst only about 8 sq. m. were found, the original area covered could have been over 500 sq. m. At least one architectural scheme, perhaps in three-dimensions and similar to some in the rooms in the Roman Painted House at Dover, was found with Period V rubbish and probably relates to Period III/IV. A simple rectilinear scheme of red and green panels had been painted onto the West Corridor wall, which collapsed early in Period V and can only have related to Periods II–IV.

The 70 fragments of window-glass, of varying types, show that glazed windows were included in the structure, probably small panes held in wooden frames. The identified floors were of *opus signinum* in the West Corridor and Room 15 (both Period II) and of clay in Room 7 (Period II). Plain red tessellation was used in Rooms 5, 11 and the East Corridor (all

Period III) and in Rooms 1, 2 and 4 (probably laid in Period III). The presence of six small coloured tesserae, could indicate that at least one room had been provided with a small mosaic panel. The floor in Room 14D (Period V) was of concrete, as probably was Room 13C (also Period V). The floors in Rooms 6, 10 and 16 were suspended over hypocausts and may also have been of concrete.

Periods I, III and V clearly represented very major building programmes. Broad calculations suggest that at least 180,000 flints may have been needed, more than 10,000 roof tiles and bricks, perhaps 600 pilae tiles, 65 bridging-tiles and some 200–270 box-flue tiles. The tessellated floors (including Room 3) would have needed more than 250,000 tesserae to cover the rooms completely.

The samian ware from the site is predominantly Antonine in date and mostly came from Central Gaul and the Argonne. The coarse pottery is again predominantly Antonine, though the later third and fourth centuries are well represented. The few coins from the site, some 96% of which are late-third or fourth century, are clearly not representative of the occupation of the site as a whole and simply represent accidental coin-loss.

It seems likely that the Roman house, with its range of rooms, flanked by corridors set in a rural landscape, was the main house of a major villa farming-estate. The form of the house is familiar in scale and content to several villas in the Kent countryside, notably at nearby Keston (Ref. 1), but also at Lullingstone (Ref. 6), Faversham (Ref. 51) and Farningham (Ref. 5). These principal houses stood adjacent to a complex of buildings, often containing granaries, outbuildings, paddocks and ovens. At nearby Keston, the only Kent villa site fully excavated, the main complex covered about two hectares and should provide a broad model for Crofton. At Keston the main complex lay on the east side of the villa in front of the house and if this applied at Crofton, as seems likely, then most will have been removed by the railway cutting and other developments.

Three important elements are certainly missing at Crofton, the granary, the bath-house and the cemetery. The granary probably stood east of the villa on a hillside contour, thus parallel with the villa house. A bath-house could have been attached to either of the damaged ends of the house, or could have been detached and some metres from it and near a source of water. Equally certain must be one or more small family cemeteries where members of the household were buried during the 250 years, or more, of occupation. These would mostly lie 50–100 m. from the main house, often on higher ground with cremations (early) and inhumations (late), the latter sometimes in small mausolea, as at Keston.

The villa estate probably changed its size and production during the 250 years of activity, perhaps reflecting the prosperity of the family at any time. It seems to have been the largest Roman building in the upper Cray Valley and it is likely that it farmed most of the surrounding area, perhaps at times in excess of 200 hectares. This would have included arable, pasture and woodland. No doubt the nearby River Cray played a major part in the agricultural activities, producing ample watering for cattle and sheep and also providing water transport for large quantities of grain. Tracks must have connected the villa to the main arterial roads within easy reach.

The villa formed part of a wider landscape that included other villas to the east, west and north. These must have been held by similar families, clearly the principal land-owners and to some extent resembling Kent estates of the post-medieval period. It seems very likely that these families were known to each other and of a similar social standing. Together they held a very large area of land, probably provided some of the senior officials in local government and their children inter-married. They must have shared common problems such as inflation, variable crops and of course the end of Roman Britain.

E. THE POST ROMAN PERIOD

On the final abandonment of the villa the tiles slid from the roof of the Period V house and formed large heaps on the west side, where they were buried by deep layers of hillwash from the slope above. The structural walls were subsequently heavily robbed, perhaps in part to help build Orpington church and only survived to a maximum height of 1.12 m. No later than the 11th century some 40–60 cm. of sterile hillwash covered most of the villa. About then a substantial pit was cut into the hillwash and just into the Roman terraces below. This contained two domestic hearths, perhaps bread ovens, which had been covered with burnt daub from a nearby structure. The pottery from it was of 11–12th century date and it is possible that this pit was dug within a structure of which no other traces survive.

Nearby were two post-holes, one containing a sherd of a 14th century jug, which clearly post-dated the hearth-pit and may have formed part of a structure of unknown site. These three features clearly relate to the use of the site in medieval times and could represent one of the manors recorded in the Domesday Survey (Ref. 52) as 'Croctune', but never found. Ideally, Crofton should lie about 400 m. to the west beyond the hillcrest where the name now predominates and is shown on early maps. The Survey states that Croctune covered a sulung and a yoke, which is over 200 acres and it could thus extend down the slope to the Roman site. It is certainly the best available candidate now and it is surely not a coincidence that it occupied the Roman site, as so often elsewhere.

The documentary evidence here is also interesting, though as always this must be treated with some caution. An early charter of 973 (BCS 1295) refers to 'crop tunes' and this is taken by some (Ref. 54) to be Crofton. The root element here is taken to be Old English for 'rounded place' and the second element as 'farmstead'. Hence, *farmstead on a low mound*. This might just fit the villa site for the debris of the Roman house would have formed a low mound. Certainly the name in Domesday in 1086 was Croctune and it is possible that this is the evolved form of 'crop tunes'. If in fact Croctune was the original name of the site then the root would change to 'crock, or pottery'. This would then produce *farmstead on the pottery place*. Whilst both names could reflect the ruins of the villa, the latter is more attractive in that the Roman site certainly contained very large amounts of pottery and tile! Either way, the name had evolved to Crofton by 1240 and still remains in constant use in 1995.

BIBLIOGRAPHICAL REFERENCES

Ref. No.	Subject	Author	Publication
1	Keston Villa	Philp, B. et al	*The Roman Villa Site at Keston* (1991), (Kent Monograph No. 6).
2	Fordcroft Site	Philp, B. and Keller, P.	*The Roman Site at Fordcroft, Orpington* (1995) (KSSS No. 8).
3	Darenth Villa	Philp, B.	*Excavations in West Kent 1960–70* (1973) p. 119 (Kent Monograph No. 2).
4	Horton Kirby Villa	Philp, B and Mills, R.	*The Roman Villa Site at Horton Kirby, Kent.* (1991) (KSSS No. 5).
5	Farningham Villa	Meates, G.	*Arch. Cant.* LXXXVIII (1973), p. 1.
6	Lullingstone Villa	Meates, G.	*The Lullingstone Roman Villa* (1980).
7	Discovery	–	*J.R.S.* Vol. XVII (1927), p. 209
8	Discovery	–	*Arch. Cant.* XL (1928), *xlvi*.
9	Discovery	Elliston-Erwood, F.C.	*Arch. Cant.* LXVIII (1954), p. 207.
10	Excavation	Parsons, J.	*Arch. Cant.* LXXI (1957), p. 240.
11	Excavation	Parsons, J.	*Arch. Cant.* LXXII (1958), p. 210.
12	Excavation	Parsons, J.	*Arch. Cant.* LXXIII (1959), 1.
13	Report	Parsons, J.	*Archives* (O.D.A.S.), Vol. 3 (No. 2).
14	Report	Philp, B.	*K.A.R.* No. 78 (1984), p. 196
15	Excavation	Philp, B.	*K.A.R.* No. 94 (1988), p. 74
16	Award	Philp, B.	*K.A.R.* No. 95 (1989), p. 108
17	Preservation Scheme	Philp, B.	*K.A.R.* No. 101 (1990), p. 1
18	Preservation Scheme	Mynott, E.	*K.A.R.* No. 103 (1991), p. 67
19	Opening Villa	–	*K.A.R.* No. 110 (1992), p. 221
20	Awards	–	*K.A.R.* No. 119 (1995), p. 204
21	Bronze Ring, No. 2	Henig, M.	*A Corpus of Roman Engraved Gemstones from British Sites*, BAR 8 (1974), No. 763.
22	Toothpick, No. 9	Johns, C and Bland, R.	*Brit.* XXV (1994), p. 172
23	Bone Pin, No. 16	Crummy, N.	The Roman Small Finds from the Excavations at Colchester, (1983), No. 309
24	Samian Ware	Hermet, F.	*La Graufesenque (Condatomago)* (1934) (Paris, reprinted Marseille 1979).
25	Samian Ware	Ricken, H. and Fischer, C.	*Die Bilderschüsseln der römischen Töpfer von Rheinzabern. Textband mit Typenbildern zu Katalog VI der Ausgrabungen von Wilhelm Ludowici in Rheinzabern 1901–1914*, Materialen zur römischgermanischen Keramik, Heft 7 (Bonn), (1963).
26	Samian Ware	Rogers, G.B.	*Les poteries sigillees de la Gaule Centrale, I: les motifs non figurés*, Gallia Supplement 28 (Paris) (1974).
27	Samian Ware	Stanfield, J.A. and Simpson, G.	*Les potiers de la Gaule Centrale*, Recherches sue les Ateliers de Potiers de la Gaule Centrale, Tomes 5/Revue Archéologique Sites, Hors-série 37, (1990) (Gonfaron).
28	Samian Stamp	Curle, J.	*A Roman Frontier Post and its People, The Fort of Newstead.* Glasgow. (1911).
29	Samian Stamp	Forster, R.H.	'Corstopitum. Report of the excavations in 1907.'. *Arch. Ael.* 3 ser. 6, p. 205–303. (1908).
30	Samian Stamp	Stansfield, J.A. and Simpson, G.	*Central Gaulist Potters*, London. (1958).
31	Samian Stamp	Ulbert, G.	*Das frührömische Kastell Rheingönheim.* Limesforschungen 9, Berlin. (1969).
32	Mortaria	Bennett, P. Frere, S. and Stow, S.	*The Archaeology of Canterbury, vol. I: Excavations at Canterbury Castle*, Canterbury Archaeological Trust, Maidstone, (1982).

BIBLIOGRAPHICAL REFERENCES

33	Mortaria	Frere, S.	*Verulamium Excavations*, Volume I. Rept. Res. Comm. of Soc. of Ants. of London, No. XXVIII, Oxford, (1972). Hartley, K. 'The Mortarium stamps', p. 371–81.
34	Mortaria	Frere, S.	*Verulamium Excavations*, Volume II. Rept. Res. Comm. of Soc. of Ants. of London. No. XLI, London, (1983).
35	Mortaria	Frere, S.	*Verulamium Excavations*, Volume III. Oxford University Comm. for Arch. Monograph No. 1, Oxford, (1984).
36	Mortaria	Holbrook, N. and Bidwell, P.	*Roman Finds from Exeter*, Exeter Arch. Repts., No. 4, Exeter, (1991).
37	Mortaria	Hull, M.R.	*The Roman Potters' Kilns of Colchester*. Repts. Res. Comm. Antiq. London, No. XXI. Oxford, (1963).
38	Mortaria	Young, C.	*The Roman Pottery Industry of the Oxford Region*, BAR 43. Oxford, (1977).
39	Coarse Pottery	Lyne, M. and Jefferies R.S.	*The Alice Holt/Farnham Roman Pottery Industry*, CBA Rep. 30, (1979).
40	Coarse Pottery	Philp, B.	*The Excavation of the Roman Forts of the Classis Britannica at Dover*, 1970–77 (1981). (Kent Monograph No. 3).
41	Coarse Pottery	Philp, B.	*The Roman House with Bacchic Murals at Dover* (1989). (Kent Monograph No. 5).
42	Coarse Pottery	Philp, B.	*Excavations in the Darent Valley* (1984). (Kent Monograph No. 4).
43	Coarse Pottery	Philp, B.	See Ref. 1.
44	Coarse Pottery	Monaghan, J.	*Upchurch and Thameside Roman Pottery*, BAR 173, (1987).
45	Coarse Pottery	Monaghan, J.	See Ref. 44.
46	Coarse Pottery	Pollard, R.	*The Roman Pottery of Kent*, (1988).
47	Coarse Pottery	Philp, B.	See Ref. 3.
48	Coarse Pottery	Young, C.	See Ref. 38.
49	Plaster	Philp, B.	See Ref. 41.
50	Station Approach	Philp, B. and Chenery, M.	*Excavation of a Roman Site at Station Approach, Orpington, 1993–4*, (1994), K.M.S.S. No. 8.
51	Faversham villa	Philp, B.	*Excavations at Faversham, 1965* (1968), p. 62.
52	Domesday Survey	Page, W. (Ed).	*Victoria County Histories (Kent)*, Vol. III (1932), p. 224a.
53	Sheep/goat burial	Philp, B.	Brit. IX (1977), p.1.
54	Place-names	Wallenberg, J	*Kentish Place-Names*, (1934), p. 300.

INDEX

Acknowledgements 8
Anglo-Saxon 2, 53
Arcadius (A.D. 395–408) 2, 34, 36, 52, 93
Archive (for site) 4
Awards 7

Barbarous Radiate 19, 25
Baxter & Co. 4
Brenchley, Viscount Monckton of 5
British Archaeological Awards 7
Bromley and West Kent Archaeological Group 4, 7, 8
Bromley Borough Council 4, 5, 7, 8
Bromley Museum 4, 87
Building Materials 88–89
    Beams 14
    Box-flue tiles 89
    Floor joists 14
    Pilae tiles 89
    Planks 14
    Roof tiles 88
    Wall tiles 89
Burials 16, 48, 94

Carausius, (A.D. 287–293) 52
Chalk Foundations 2, 10, 11, 12, 13, 14, 16, 19, 22, 91
Civic Halls 4
Coins 2, 19, 25, 34, 36, 52, 55, 93, 94
Constans, (A.D. 337–350) 52
Constantius II (A.D. 355–360) 52
Cook, Mr. Norman 53
Council for Kentish Archaeology 4, 5
Cover Building 7
Croctune 53, 95

Darenth 1, 78, 93
Domesday Survey 53, 95
Dover (also see Painted House) 78

English Heritage 4, 5, 8
Erwood, Mr. F.C.E. 2, 4, 21

Farningham 1, 94
Faversham 94
Fordcroft, Orpington 1, 40
Fordyce, Mr. A. 87
Friends of C.K.A. 5

Gallienus, (A.D. 260–268) 25
George V, (A.D. 1910–1935) 52
Glazed Windows 15, 17, 87, 91, 93

Grant, Mr. P. 5
Gratian, (A.D. 367–383) 52

Hadrian, (A.D. 117–138) 36
Horton Kirby 1, 93
Hypocaust 2, 10, 18, 19, 20, 21, 22, 24, 25, 26, 27, 28, 29,
    30, 32, 33, 36, 92, 94

Iron Age 2

K.A.R.U. 4, 5, 7, 91
Keller, Mr. P, 80
Kent Archaeological Trust 7
Keston 1, 40, 90, 93, 94

Londinium 1, 16
Lullingstone 1, 4, 94
Lynwood House 4

Marble 87
Medieval – pottery 52, 53, 80, 95
      – structure 53
Mortaria 14, 15, 24, 34, 51, 69, 70, 71
Mosaic 89, 94

North Downs 1

Opening (to the public) 7
Opus Signinum 12, 13, 14, 15, 16, 17, 18, 19, 20, 21, 23,
    24, 50, 80, 91, 92, 93
Orpington and District Archaeological Society 4, 8
Orpington Church 95
Orpington Historical Records and Natural History Society 2

Painted House, Dover 82, 87, 93
Painted Plaster (see wall plaster)
Parsons, Mr. J. 2, 4, 5
Paw Prints 32
Pentice Roof 19
Pickingtons Lane 1
Pottery
    Alice Holt 73, 75, 77
    Argonne 15
    Colchester 69, 78
    Farnham 14, 29, 34, 36
    Grog-tempered 10, 17, 34, 38
    Highgate Wood 73, 77, 78
    Much Hadham 69
    Nene Valley 75, 78
    Oxfordshire 34, 69, 75, 77

    Patch Grove 10, 15, 17, 20, 38, 45, 73, 75, 77, 78
    Rhenish 73
    Shell-loaded ware 10, 53
Porch 23
Post Holes 15, 17, 36, 40, 43, 45, 46, 50, 53

Quern 87

Reculver 4, 16
River Cray 1, 90, 94
River Darent 1, 90
River Medway 90
River Ravensbourne 1
River Thames 1

Samian 5, 10, 11, 14, 15, 17, 23, 24, 25, 33, 34, 40, 43, 51, 52, 62–68, 94
Samian – Potter's stamps 62, 63, 64, 65, 66, 67, 68
Saxon (see Anglo-Saxon)
Small Finds
    Antler 49
    Bone 5, 15, 25, 33, 48, 49, 51, 57, 87
    Bowl 59
    Bracelet 25, 32, 34, 57, 59
    Bronze 10, 15, 17, 23, 25, 33, 34, 52, 57, 87, 90
    Brooch 10, 23, 57
    Earscoop 51, 57
    Flint 5, 9, 10, 34, 40, 45, 51, 87, 88, 90
    Glass 5, 14, 15, 25, 30, 34, 48, 49, 51, 53, 59, 87
    Hone 59
    Iron 49, 87
    Jet and Shale 14, 32, 51, 59
    Key 57
    Lead 87
    Ligula 57
    Marked chalk block 33
    Mount 57
    Nail 57
    Needle 57, 59
    Pin 17, 25, 33, 51, 57, 59
    Rake 59
    Ring 34, 57
    Spoon 59
    Stone 9, 10, 15, 59
    Tablet 59
    Toothpick/ear-cleaner 34, 57
    Tweezers 52, 57
Specialists 8
Springhead 4
Stanbrook, Mr. I. (M.P.) 5
Station Approach, Orpington 91

Tank/bath 22, 23
Tessellated floor 19, 22, 23, 25, 88
Tesserae 5, 12, 13, 20, 21, 23, 24, 30, 33, 34, 88, 89, 92, 94
Thanet Beds 10
Theodosius (A.D. 379–395), 36, 93

Upper Chalk 88

Valens, (A.D. 364–378) 34
Valentinian I, (A.D. 364–375) 34, 36
Veranda 19

Wall plaster 14, 24, 25, 49, 80–87, 93
Warbank, Keston 1, 40, 90, 93, 94
Well shafts 2, 34–36, 93

PLATES

Plate II Members of the public being given guided tours of the site, July, 1988.

Plate III   The rammed chalk foundations in Room 2 (Period I).

Plate IV   Section of collapsed wall of the West Corridor (by Room 7) sealing fallen roof tiles.

Plate V Detail of splayed window-opening in collapsed West Corridor wall.

Plate VI The north-west corner of Room 15, later cut by the Period V wall of Room 16 (at top).

Plate VII   Room 8, showing rammed chalk foundations (Period I), floor (Period II), side walls (Period III), fallen roof tiles and Shaft F 51 (bottom left).

Plate VIII   Room 9 from the north-east, showing west wall and floor (Period II), east wall (Period III) and south wall and stoke-hole (both Period V).

Plate IX Detail showing rammed chalk foundations (Period I) under flint wall (Period III) on west side of Room 4.

Plate X Detail of tiled base in stoke-hole Room 9.

Plate XI   Detail showing surviving area of tessellated floor in Room 11 (Period III).

Plate XII   South-west corner (with tiles) of Room 14C (Period IV) cutting through the south wall of Room 15 (Period II).

Plate XIII General view from the north-east showing Rooms 11 (foreground), 13B (left), 14D (top), during Period V.

Plate XIV General view from the east showing Rooms 5 (foreground), 6 (centre), 10 (top), 16 (top left) and 11 (left), during Period V.

Plate XV Room 6B (Period V) from the north-east showing hypocaust channels.

Plate XVI Room 10 (Period V) from the south-west showing pilae and main flue openings.

Plate XVII Detail of north-west corner of Room 10 (Period V) showing pilae stacks, arched opening (right) and wall flues.

Plate XVIII Detail showing tiled offset and box-flue tile in west wall of Room 10 (Period V).

Plate XIX Room 16 (Period V) from the west showing dwarf walls and main flue (on left).

Plate XX General view of surviving channelled hypocaust in Room 13B (Period V) from the north-west.

Plate XXI   Detail of hypocaust channels in Room 13B (Period V) showing chalk blocks and tiles.

Plate XXII   General view of Room 14D (Period V) from the north-west showing substantially complete hypocaust system.

Plate XXIII Detail showing tiles covering the hypocaust channels at the centre of Room 14D (Period V).

Plate XXIV Detail showing animal paw-prints on tiles built into the hypocaust in Room 14D (Period V).

Plate XXV The West Ditch (fourth century) from the east, showing re-cut and earlier adjacent features (left).

Plate XXVI Shaft F 51 (fourth century) fully excavated, cutting through the north wall of Room 8 (Period III).

Plate XXVII Pit-Line B from the east, cutting through Gully F21, with Pit-Line C (left) and West Ditch (right).

Plate XXVIII Detail showing area of fallen roof-tiles on west side of villa outside Room 9.

Plate XXIX Detail showing section across 11–12th century hearth cut into hillwash layers sealing the Roman villa, with Post Hole F26 in foreground.